"*The Caving Grounds* is one of the most original books I've ever read. It is partly an impressionistic history of actual caving grounds, but it is much more than that. There is weeping here. There is wild humor, passion, and mystery. The narrator sometimes resembles the 'feral grandchild' mentioned in one of the poems: wild, untamed, singing at the top of her lungs. But more often she aches for the caving ground, aches with the stories she sings to us, for all that has been destroyed and for the beauty of life somehow preserved. This is an amazing and unforgettable book."

—Jim Moore, author of *Underground* and *Prognosis*

"In Kathleen Heideman, Upper Michigan's wild woods and creatures and old timber towns and mining communities and rich but wounded earth itself have found one of their truest poetic voices. Hers is work that both sings and heals the place that births it. Freighted deep with Heideman's vast natural, cultural, ecological, historical, and—above all—local knowledge, *The Caving Grounds* adds to my great adoration (and, yes, delighted mythologization) of this poet of the Yellow Dog River wilds."

—Jonathan Johnson, author of
In the Land We Imagined Ourselves and *The Desk on the Sea*

"'It all begins with loss,' Kathleen Heideman declares, and she warns that 'You better wear long sleeves / when you enter our sunken places.' Her poems will make you tremble at the destruction wrought: the caving ground that swallows a town; the poisons left behind by mining. In a prodigious act of mythmaking, the poet has begun the difficult work of mending our greedy past, probing the most intimate pockets of place and history. Innovation marks her work as extraordinary. Her imagination shows us how to mourn and love."

—Todd Davis, author of *Ditch Memory: New & Selected Poems*

"Kathleen Heideman has written a heartbreaking exegesis of the gutted iron mining communities of the Upper Peninsula. *The Caving Grounds* is simultaneously loving and damning, hallucinatory and erudite, playful and ruthless."

—Marcia Bjornerud, author of *Turning to Stone*
and *Timefulness: How Thinking Like a Geologist Can Help Save the World*

"Kathleen M. Heideman takes the reader on a fascinating journey through the unstable, sinking landscape in upper Michigan where the underground mine shafts slowly collapse. This landscape near Lake Superior had a soft and rich ore body with many unusual features. Her guide is Rusty, a drinker and a daredevil who travels the danger zones where people, houses, and herds of cattle have been lost. With Rusty and other residents, she descends into the past through virgin forests, indigenous knowledge, and strong headwinds of economic development that lead to depletion. She travels underground, much the same as going down to Hades to witness the clammy workplaces that never would see the sun. There are some shafts that have trapped and entombed their workers, and some with air toxic to breathe.

The Caving Grounds is an excellent read. The poetic forms are novel and engaging, and the language is often musical. She brings to us stories full of entertaining bar talk and harrowing tales of life and death, both heroic and foolish. There are details of the protozoic era and the surprising properties of magnetic fields. While this is an important documentation of a mining community, it is a story told with humor and insight. This is also a singing, an ancient song-story about resilience, about men who descended into the earth, women who patched broken lives, and mining companies that made their profits and departed. Heideman has woven an epic tale. This story of the working class, the beginning and aftermath of iron mines, and of human strength and vulnerability is set in the context of myth, human history, and literature. Heideman's images are riveting, and her connections grant us a larger view of past and future. This is a great literary achievement."

—Sheila Packa, former Duluth Poet Laureate, author of
Night Train Red Dust: Poems of the Iron Range and *Surface Displacements*

"The poems in Kathleen Heideman's *The Caving Grounds* unfold 'accordion-style': they constrict, fold in, crackle, and breathe out the history of Negaunee. As poems explore 'the delineation of the orebody,' how 'these lands are pocked with holes that swallow anecdotal evidence,' Heideman unearths the narrative, blending her position as poet-investigator to ensure a grand effort in crafting a 'Complete History / of the Terrain in question.' 'O the lichens have their work cut out for them / forgetting our names!' is a brave challenge, as Heideman balances the preservation of this town's rich history through her earthy observations. And yet, how precise can our 'metaphors of labor' be in our language, while still listening to the 'mouth of the mineshaft'? Heideman's poems give support and structure to keep these voices and land alive."

—Carly Joy Miller, author of *Ceremonial* and *Like a Beast*

"In *The Caving Grounds*, Kathleen Heideman memorably marries poetry and history, labor and geology, as she goes down into the old mines beneath Negaunee, in Michigan's Upper Peninsula. Sometimes she has a guide, her own Virgil, as she peels back the history and geology, until she arrives at the oldest fossils in the world. She can't escape the work she has to do, but it's hard!

I don't want to sing this anymore!
My heart has a verse to deliver, but I am weary of delivering it,
weary of moss, rusty skips, rotten boards over holes.

But she comes back to the people, the old ones who give her the necessary stories of the work and the place. She comes back to the land and the Lakes, even as the ground caves into the abandoned mines below her. The rest of us must be grateful that she has found the verse and delivered it, creating a poem both profoundly researched and deeply felt."

—Keith Taylor, author of *All the Time You Want* and *The Bird-while*

THE CAVING GROUNDS

A Brief Report on the Human Animal

Psalms of the Early Anthropocene

THE CAVING GROUNDS

Kathleen M. Heideman

Modern History Press
Ann Arbor, MI

Library of Congress Cataloging-in-Publication Data

Names: Heideman, Kathleen M., 1968- author.
Title: The caving grounds / Kathleen M. Heideman.
Description: Ann Arbor, MI : Modern History Press, [2024] | Summary: "This
    poetry collection, deeply grounded in research and interviews, explores
    the history of iron mining in Negaunee, Michigan through a chorus of
    storytellers. The title "The Caving Grounds" refers to the undermined,
    abandoned neighborhoods left behind, some of which remain fenced and
    dangerous, as well as the broader sociocultural impacts of mining in the
    Upper Peninsula"-- Provided by publisher.
Identifiers: LCCN 2024041655 (print) | LCCN 2024041656 (ebook) | ISBN
    9781615998463 (hardcover) | ISBN 9781615998456 (paperback) | ISBN
    9781615998470 (adobe pdf)
Subjects: LCSH: Iron mines and mining--Michigan--Negaunee--Poetry. |
    Negaunee (Mich.)--Poetry. | LCGFT: Poetry.
Classification: LCC PS3608.E3573 C38 2024 (print) | LCC PS3608.E3573
    (ebook) | DDC 811/.6--dc23/eng/20240924
LC record available at https://lccn.loc.gov/2024041655
LC ebook record available at https://lccn.loc.gov/2024041656

Book #2 in the Yooper Poetry Series

ISBN 978-1-61599-846-3 hardcover
ISBN 978-1-61599-845-6 paperback
ISBN 978-1-61599-847-0 ebook

Cover design by Mona Z. Kraculdy
Cover art photograph by Kristina Wilson
Author photograph by Pamela Arnold

Published by
Modern History Press   www.ModernHistoryPress.com
5145 Pontiac Trail   info@ModernHistoryPress.com
Ann Arbor, MI 48105   Toll-free 888-761-6268

Distributed by Ingram Group (USA/CAN/AU/EU)

*For my profoundly creative mother Doris,
for my dear husband Daniel, who believes,
and for Rebecca, who always said, "Go."*

*

"Start a huge, foolish project, like Noah. It makes
absolutely no difference what people think of you."[1]

CONTENTS[2]

I.

II.

III.

IV.

V.

I.

The place for the rendezvous of ideas is underground.[3]

of which "no stirring words were ever spoken."[4]

So I gave up fact and went to myth ...[5]

NOW PLAYING

Down at the Delft Theatre we're all watching that silent film, *Taming the Michigan Wilderness*, for the umpteenth time. When it's done, the projectionist plays it backwards, to rewind, & everyone stays to watch that too, even better, like it was a vaudeville Magician's act — O how astonishing! — to see our black trains running backwards uphill from the oredocks, engines swallowing smoke, broken ore pouring out from trams, back down shaft[6] holes where it came from, our grandfathers unbent & growing younger, smiling now, the roads un-ribboning, replaced by ferns & upholstered slopes of pin-cushion moss, the Miner's Bank & Trust building disassembled, dragged stone by stone back to the quarry & best of all, great logs rolling uphill from the riverbanks, bouncing a few times like boys on a diving board, and bounding upright: White Pines! White Pines! Wild-haired virgins! Pine trees, ancient trees, far as the eye can see!

PREFATORY QUIZ TO HELP READERS TO GAUGE THE DEPTHS OF THEIR OWN UNDERSTANDING

Kindly fill each void with an answer:

1. The Reader is urged to proceed with care as there are few reliable maps
2. for the void is vug, is gravity-flattened drift, is a blank to be filled
3. The Place was mostly unmapped, still _____
4. When seeing peculiar fluctuations in his _____ _____, surveyor W. A. Burt directed his men "*Seek the Cause*"
5. The Place was Negaunee, home of Beaver, Bear, Crane, Moose and _____
6. They returned with chunks of _____ _____, pulled from local _____
7. Soon, more men arrived at the mouth of the river, and hired the Anishinaabe _____ Maji-gesik to *show the Place to them*
8. He was reluctant, walked _____ as he neared the Place
9. Maji-gesik said it was _____, an outcrop *where* _____ *often struck!*
10. He showed them _____ _____ in the upturned roots of a white _____
11. By year's end, there were more than _____ Mining _____
12. The white pine was cut and dragged underground!
13. The _____ _____ _____ _____ birthed hundreds of open pits and _____ _____ during the coming century, until easy ore was gone
14. For 150 years, the Place was _____ and _____
15. Whole sections of _____ began sinking and _____ due to the removal of a soft _____
16. Place was utterly exhausted[7], _____, _____ and _____
17. We stand together now in the mine's first _____, not too far down
18. Geological pressures push the ceiling rock lower, displacing hollow _____
19. Water floods most of the old mine _____
20. What we recall is _____ like rock; iron stains the creases in our hands
21. May we extract only _____ memories, then cease remembering?
22. No. "*Hado, ano, kato*" wrote Heraclitus, roughly meaning: *we must imagine ourselves standing astride a battered ore-bucket, lowered into the* _____, *for the path* _____ *and the path* _____ *are the* _____ *path*

KEY: wilderness, magnetic compass, Wolf, specular hematite, outcrops, guide, backward, sacred, lightning, iron, sparkling, pine, 100, Companies, Lake Superior Iron Range, underground mines, booming, profitable, Negaunee, subsiding, orebody, undermined, abandoned, fenced, level, drifts, workings, fractured, untarnished, earth, up, down, same

4

"LET THERE BE LIGHT," SAYS THE DRILL BIT, BREAKING THROUGH

For it is best to see like a Child, still
discovering, far better to be a Child at play
than play the Expert;
best to be ecstatic each morning, a flower dumb-struck by light —
flinging yourself open to the obvious, cracked stone, a rescue
party with their headlamps shouting and pointing or stricken,
standing in a crowd with your mouth an open cave of awe,
O! making wide the petals of your eyes, soaking in the miracle
the rest have grown accustomed to, *light* —

" * "

for the *Sun is always Shining*
we are reminded in *The Child's True Book of Weather*
— it is shining even while we are mining iron
a thousand feet underground
or when we sleep in dark rooms
exiled from light, when we're old and cataract'd,
sun dimmed to asterisk, or if we flee billowing catastrophe,
or during blizzards or fog, we must remember —
it shines still and ever will, Light
in the window of our neighbor's house,
in the Teacher's library, beyond the continent's edge,
in the hour after the cave-in, in black spruce boughs;
Let there be Light, says the drill bit, breaking through
and rescuing the miners
for it is always shining
even when we haven't seen the sun for years,
through all the clouds, all our tears.

FATHER VAARAMÄKI'S HOMILY

Poor Negaunee, so pure with snow, freshly white-washed, so studded with taverns and steeples and shaft heads, iron-stained as any butcher shop, and Father Vaaramäki[8], who meant to say "sacrament" tonight and stood there blank-tongued in the middle of the Mass, dumbstruck, moonlight leaking from every hole in his head. Silent minutes passed; we worried he was having a stroke — then he opened his mouth and homily poured out: O how the iron range glows and shimmers in Thy falling snow, luminous with well-scrubbed faithful, the white-sugared optimism of mine workings, ore dusted with snow! Must I mention failure or fracture here, this blessed night? I say no! No. For even X waits to deliver bad news, even catastrophe demurs, hangs back like a wolf at the edge of a clearing until Thy deer have ponded like Job floundering in deep snow. Progress! Industry! Optimism! Open the ledgers! Boughs greening our mantles while outside, the spruce grouse thrums and chews her meager needles! Bring out sour black bread and break it, share Thy bounty, Thy juustoa and blood-sausages and pickled pig's feet! Thy wine is sweet, Thy wind is bitter. Let bacon-drippings be spread on sacramental wafers for every poor man tonight, and poor babes too, for it is Christmas Eve, a rare full moon swoops low to smile upon our town — grant now our dumb beasts the gift of speech, let the cow and kitten deliver prophecies, let the rooster forecast record profits in the coming year, X-many million tons of ore shipped, X-many stopes emptied. Now let us raise our voice in prayer, let us crank the Victrola and sing, for when we sing we are not poor, we are not hollowed, we are holy! And if we cannot be holy, let us cross ourselves and be certain of that fact — that in X's name we tremble, in X's name make amends.

A POCKET GUIDE TO THE CAVING GROUNDS[9]

Aeons and aeons of rock.
They are too tongueless to tell
the gist of their long endurance.[10]

According to cartographers, anything we can
spatially imagine may be mapped, even places we
will never go, the Moon, the Milky Way, *imaginary places*
such as purgatory, mind-maps, Territory of Love[11],
water-filled shafts under Main Street —

⚒

Or say Negaunee's unpredictable body is muscled here,
fat there, a random whorling between these extremes,
dots to mark where she was undermined by generations,
dots for softness, for grandfathers-fathers-sons,
dots to mark cemeteries, bodies never found,
dots to mark spots where her ruined features
spell Braille warnings: caving grounds, mappable

. ::....
.. .. :: ....
..... ::..... ..:: .. .. ::...
.. ..::. ....::. ....::. :.. ...

dots on the map say overburden
turning back where bedrock veins
writhe black along Teal Lake's far pink flank,
impenetrable, adjusting her surfaces to fit the varying
delineations of low-lands, orebodies, bluff-curves —
granular patterns
materializing as the out-of-town granddaughter
takes a careful grave-rubbing from leaning slabs,
simple markers for hard lives half-remembered;

She is whatever you track
into the house, a gritty woman common as dirt —
whatever grips the tread of your sole
or catches in the neck folds of a sleeping body,
moist whetstone for your mother's pain,
sharpening each feature. The map legend promises
swamps and hills and more: virginstone,
motherlode, rockfaces south of town
where the county roadcrew blew a four-lane hole
through her hardened heart, her outcrop —

her face Precambrian, Archean, Banded Iron Formation,
a mottled 55-mph blur of pink and blue-gray
defaced by the naive arithmetic of u+me4ever —
specularite, cornerstone,
the Miners Bank reborn as Union Headquarters,
sandstone whose eroding surface reveals vines, distant artisan's hand.

She is your inner landscape populated by minutia:
whatever shape lichen takes
colonizing a monument, whatever turns the lake water green
or grows in rain-rinsed crevices, whatever mosses homestead
the lips of abandoned shafts

⚒

whatever miniature sedge
or columbine struggle-blossoms on a high ledge,
whatever form she takes she is your mother's mother,
name-lines set in limestone,
a memorial of banded jaspillite and specularite,
the birth and deathlines of her, each etched headstone letter
grown thin on a diet of winter weather —
she is ironwork, ruined forge, iron bluffs flowering on topo maps

```
 \\ || //
>       <
 // || \\
```

ruined castle towers of stone guarding weariness —
she is the mine-town shuddering daily
at a quarter-past, internal clockwork, subterranean
blasts from which structures reverberate but go on standing,
swayed turret-stone in the defense of her own nature, strong —
she is iron mixed with bentonite mixed with lime —
pelletized and improved-upon for industry's sake,
taconite mask a woman applies to hide softer thoughts —
birthstone, crystallized, born in voids

her bones are limestone, dolomite, headstone, rubblestone,
Miner's last cave-in, Mud-in-your-eye,
The Only Lawn a Man Need Never Mow,
Oracle stone, sandy meadow strewn with angels, dates, lichens,
ivy, plastic mums, raw spots where the earth
was so recently disturbed

According to the map, she's the last turn
at the end of a long dirt road, dead end,
Lodestone Motel — Madame Geologie, Proprietress
a democratic resting place for laborers
and laggards alike, all requests for lake-view suites honored,
offering hard beds for the faithful
and hard beds for adulterers, all wages equal
under her gravel-roofed graves.

CERTAIN THINGS YOU SHOULD KNOW ABOUT RUSTY

Rusty hasn't come home. His truck's behind the Crow Bar
but nobody's heard from him for a week.
He's probably just gone down, Rusty's ma says, gesturing vaguely.
Where — down in the basement? I say. I'm weary,
I'm tired of these games Rusty plays.
Down south? Down 'the bottom of Lake Superior? Down to Hades?
Don't be smart, she says, looking sideways. She runs her iron
up and down her blouse, until I can smell the hot cotton.
Then softer: the Old Location.

I'm the outsider. To be an insider,
you need to know the difference between "new location"
and "old location." Your family's
bones need to have been buried, east of town,
dug up, and reburied a second time down by the Carp River.

She hands me a tattered flier. Read, she says.
It looks like a truck tire ran over it, embossed with gravel,
something saved from Pioneer Days, when she staffed
the Chamber of Commerce Information Desk and wore her name
on a plastic tag pinned above her heart — *Laurentia Maki — Just Ask Me!*
It's a well known fact that Laurie dislikes tourists.
they ask such dumb questions, really, and their cameras click-click
click over every mundane thing — little bites out of the world, she says,
oohing and aahing at every roadside apple, but they take two bites
and spit you out, soon as they spot the wormhole. Laurie
looks me up and down, not one bit motherly.

Certain things you should know about Rusty, she warns.

> On this spot on Sept 19, 1844, William A. Burt was the first to discover the great
> Lake Superior iron ore deposits. Peculiar fluctuations in his magnetic compass led
> Burt to ask his men to seek the cause; they soon returned with pieces of iron ore from
> outcroppings in the area … Maji-gesik, a Chippewa chief guided members of the
> party in the summer to this region and showed them the iron ore in the roots of a
> fallen pine tree. By 1846, there were 106 mining companies.[12]

Mrs. Maki's sacred local history text! Amen, I laugh

under my breath. Then I see, scrawled on the other side,
the note Rusty left for me.

⚒

Believable? This Russell "hell-everybody-calls-me-Rusty"
— these words really come from his lips?
His actions —
        plausible?
You love him?

Consider his education level, his motivations, societal norms,
the breathable atmosphere of an old mining town smothering his hope,
withering in his chest like a neglected houseplant,
last summer's geraniums in an upstairs window,
just enough December light for a few spindly leaves, a bloom.

That's Rusty for you. Can't kill him — he flowers,
can't keep him from stealing any scene
he enters: *life of the party tonight, Rusty!*
— though he's just as likely to scowl for days,
slam doors, fill his old army pack with dried venison,
flour, canned goods, brandy in a plastic water jug,
and drive, come dawn, down a two-track.

Sometimes he abandons his truck behind a bar or at a gate,
sometimes he leaves it buried to the fender in mud,
hikes the rest of the way in to some collapsing shack in a swamp
or on the rim of an old shaft where he may or may not break in,
fall asleep to the whine of mosquitos,
though he's a good shot, repairs the window-screen
with needle and thread, smiles to see the sliver of a moon.

How easily he forgets work, time, you,
swears off all humans for a month at a clip.
Not like he's in the arms of another woman, so it's possible.
But a month? O Rusty, that's pushing it a bit, I think.

⚒

Looking up at the Miners Bank building
as a thin slice of yellow moon
"swam out from behind a jagged dark cliff"
by which we meant the clouds passed an outcrop
revealing the moon. Some time back, Maji-gesik
agreed to guide strangers to a place near Negaunee
where stones were banded red and silver,
where iron like stars shone from upturned roots.

He didn't approach the tree himself, he pointed with his chin,
didn't point at it with a finger,
he walked backward as they neared it.

Thanks! said Ohio, salivating over the scene.
Hey, I'm just showing you, I'm not
giving it away or anything, said Maji-gesik,
but it was too late.
Have you seen kids go wild, unwrapping presents?
Drills and sledges wedged their foot in the door,
ribboned open every crack, pits and drifts and shafts
pushed down, declared the whole Range
Open for Business!

Larger than myself, Desire, this fragrant orange,
this great Magnet calling iron filings to itself,
O! Rusty, bite into me, drill me, tug me closer —

Who's been down there lately? Who's down there now?
Rusty, that you?

Who's on first, who's on second? Who's unaccounted for?
Cap'n Merry says a man's brass check is missing from the board.

Who's on second? You tell me who's on second, damnit, I'm done, I'm wrung!

Who's to say the ore's exhausted? — they'll be back. He'll come home, Rusty.

Who lost their dance partner? Where could that man be hiding?

Has the age of hermits passed? Who said so? Who's on first, toeing dust?
Who says there ain't maybe a wild one down the shaft, praying his prayers?

You do the math. Who's got the heavier burden:
— him with a ton of feathers, her with a ton of iron?

Who's to know what follows next or soon, a mining bust or mineral boom
or whether like orecars, we'll move unoiled against each other

coupling & uncoupling
Who's down there? she called, frightened, her mind's cellar

propped with timbers, the uneven floor dead-ending at a wall of bedrock,
Laurentian Shield, — things crawling, the wall dripping music

when it rains, a fine reminder this land's a manuscript of orogeny,
paleographic disputes, tumult older-than-the-hills, our narrative folded

accordion-style, the seams are leather, cracking, orebody exposed
and exploited, the lines / enjambed

— *Nobody,* a voice said. It sounded just like Rusty.
Nobody's been down here for forever.

THE SEA OF VICIOUS CIRCLES

Bureau of Mines has begun looking into the problems that may be encountered in mining on the moon … The program isn't aimed at finding new sources of metals and minerals for use on earth, but at opening up sources of supply for the time when man begins to inhabit the moon …[13]

You are no doubt aware that our Moon's floured bosom may soon
serve humanity as a night-luminous pit mine?

In the beginning,
only darkness, then moonlight
descended like a storm peeling off the roof, enlightenment!
— it took a while to grow accustomed to the bright.
We saw ourselves at our worst in this new light,
perfect faces of lovers appeared suddenly flawed,
blighted moons of pores, scars, blemishes.

Luna desires Mare, and vice versa, an ancient affair:
all night the ocean tries surging to her feet,
all night dry surfaces urge return, wishing water would rise,
lift waves through space, fill the holes where lunar core-samples
were extracted, lap a cratered body wet again.

Romantics, our old cartographers named each plain and crater
as though the moon, like a human body, contained mostly water:
Mare Vaporum, sea of vapors; Mare Frigoris, sea of cold;
Lacus Somniorum, great lake of dreams.

When the luminous Treatise of Sir Herschel

was first published, we heard what we wanted to believe: those marks
we could make out on the moon's pale surface were either ancient mines
or alluvial, "narrow zones of running water"
we imagined shimmering like the Nile, Dead River Basin,
the Escanaba by moonlight.
    And who hasn't wished for that?
a clear line between the dark side and whatever's lit,
a lunar stream of light created by the daily freeze-&-thaw,
a liquid line dividing illumination from blindness.

In retrospect: who could have predicted how
when men landed on the moon
        their rocket thrusters would stir strange clouds of dust
            disturbing the Sea of Tranquility?

⚒

Say it aloud, *Meridian*, let it split your throat in two. How well do you know
        that line from which our daily hours of work, study and love are calculated?
We shall dig a deep canal along the earth's skull, and fill it with green water;
        or plant an invisible road: a million trees, different species
for each mountain, desert, valley; a rippling green line spread thickly over each
        terrain. But it is difficult to think of such a line, unswerving highway across
        the World.
Our long use of the term *Meridian* has not worn it into a visible mental groove.
        It is a road bulldozed by shadow, a trick of math and light.

⚒

Magic Trick:
each night our planet is sawed
into equal halves of light and dark.
The magician's sword splits her
down the same line every time
reciting an old story about hell,
bolgia moats where damned souls
wander in circular trenches. Hell
— every miner knows Dante,
how Time, that sword-wielding demon,
keeps splitting us topnotch-to-crotch,

how we stumble on, clasping our uncoiled
bowels, to keep from tripping on them,
lacing boots and punching time clocks,
moving ore from the inbox to the outbox.
How our sword-scars close, unnoticed,
re-open each morning as we enter the pit
and sleep-walk through our shift
waist-deep in the Sea of Vicious Circles.

Mr. Magic waves his Happy Hour wand,
then we're blind drunk again, driving back-roads,
setting alarm-clocks in the dark.

Did I mention how Lady Luna got cut in two last night?
    I swear, Eino, first she was whole,
then they loaded her in that little pine box
like a coffin or a mancar, then her spine was cut in two.
Half hour later, she was standing whole again, perfect as an egg
— though the poor girl looked bewildered up there
when they pulled apart her box, her two sliced halves,
in the spotlight.

Up close, well ...
I'm sure the trick's mundane, but from here
the mind sees all sorts of things: a hard-boiled egg cut by a pocket knife,
ancient sacrifices, faces on the moon, snowy ruins of cities, red mud roads.

    — Last call! This round's on me, friend.
Ah good, here comes our swordsman again.

On Saint Valentine's eve, there's our librarian Spinster Olson
weeping in her dim room on Empire Street. Earlier, she stumbled again
    over a line from Prometheus Unbound, a healing of the earth
so profound it reanimates the moon — she knows the poem by heart
but always finds another detail, squinting at it, another rusty nail to snag
    her heart. Before the next full moon

she'll lose the last of her sight. For now she goes on reciting Dickinson,
I see thee, thinking of night-shift miners
     mucking iron beneath her feet;
  long hours after the page swims into twilight, *I see thee*
she's whispering, *I see thee better — in the Dark.*

HOW RUSTY STEPPED FORWARD TO BE MY GUIDE

We have seen the effects … Finn Alley and Swede Town are no longer here. They are either fenced off, because of caving ground, or they have already caved in. Over the years, Negaunee has even seen its dead moved to make room for more mining.[14]

A pick & hammer symbol
under a finger tracing trailheads
on any wilderness map shows
where shafts multiplied like mink
spreading hungry braille through the landscape
before there were towns named for what turned
a profit, extracted: Silver City, Copper
Harbor, Iron Mountain, Trout River, Birch.

— who'll be first to buy? Who'll get in line? Who's on first, who's on second? *I'm asking *you* who's on first. Who didn't come up when the whistle blew?* Exactly. Somebody's missing. But who?

"Stories?" said an old man sipping whiskey down at the Crow Bar. He claims these lands are pocked with holes that swallow anecdotal evidence, knows Abbott and Costello came through the range, doing their *who's-on-first* routine, selling war bonds — nobody told them how to pronounce Negaunee, so they butchered it. "O hell, I could tell you stories!"

So I wait, buy him another drink, but he doesn't. I'm out of money, running out of patience. I hitch up my skirt, step onto my chair, and everyone quits talking.

"Who," I challenge, "will step forward this inky night
& offer themselves as my Guide?"

How Rusty stepped forward?

Rusty said "let's" and I said "sure."
That's how.

Soon we were crawling together
under fences, sliding down slopes where
it seemed the earth had let out a long sigh —
summer puddles were hanging around
but ominous cracks crazed the wet meadow
cutting lengthwise between birch and pine
through an old haul-road
down the red ditch and back up, vanishing
under lush chokecherries. Cracks.

The trees were still saplings, 30 years or so —
20 feet max, slender girls. A ring of them in the center
had plunged several feet, and grew still,
an elevator of trees was stuck between floors.

Rusty pointed at too-round ponds,
sheer-sided black-bottomed subsidences,
showed me a garter snake bulging
with a frog's hind legs still kicking in the mouth
before the legs too were devoured,
down, down, twitching, sinking from view.

I shuddered, said it was terrible.
O, that's Negaunee for you, Rusty grinned.

⚒

I was a kid, said an old man — we lived by Maas Mine,
Prince Street, Cherry, Elm, other streets long swallowed.
Prince used to run clear out to the Carp before they emptied
and fenced her — O, back when I was a boy
there was a church cemetery out there — they dug it,
moved them bodies to a new cemetery east of the river,
and some grumbled, said there was no problem really,
said we was over-reacting. Later, where that old cemetery
stood, it started sinking, sank altogether maybe 80 feet
slumping in the center, sheltered, abandoned,

black with cherries. Dark flocks descended on the trees
down at the middle of the sinkhole, the old graveyard,
old trees getting ever so much extra water now,
too low for wind. It held the sun, see? a bread bowl
warmer than the rest of the land, like it was heated from
within, a fenced-off place, the fruit of that one cherry tree —
O, I remember it clear as the face of my best friend,
them cherries, so big and juicy! The land was off-limits, sure,
but we boys snuck in every year, ate stolen cherries,
black juice dripping from our lips in Caving Grounds.

II.

I Have Made a Heap of All that I could Find.[15]

the body contains enough iron to make a paperclip.[16]

The stranger took out a small thin rod of iron, and told him to give it to Rosamunda. "When she wishes to learn something, she must put it on top of her tongue."[17]

The desire to know history is a near relative of the desire to know truth, and that is where, for most of us, a pit lies waiting. It is a deep pit, overlaid with an innocent branch or two …[18]

too dark to say anything clearly, but not too dark to see.[19]

IRON STREET LANDLADY

From her I rent my time ...[20]

The staircase warns me of her kindly,
monstrous approach, maple groaning under
each careful step, each probing question;
her porch floors sag,
rusted bikes in her yard
take me nowhere.
Her rotting roof grows a garden of moss,
stained rainwater drips into my waiting
wastepaper bin.
Her light bulbs are dim, the lampshade
onion-skinned, piss-yellow'd
imitation vellum.
In her basement dwells Doubt:
the ancient dragon of a wringer-washer
and burlap sacks of potatoes
with wandering eyestalks, seeking, seeking.
My room came furnished, desk-bed-chair
and a palpable despair, stale air
sour as a carpet boiled in cabbage soup.
She provides weekly clean sheets,
my only luxury — crisp cotton
line-dried a thousand times, luminous
as a lover's skin, remembered.
Linoleum sags beneath my rust-stained claw foot tub,
each hot bath is a measured risk I take.
When I type all night, I feel her eye at my keyhole,
if I laugh to myself she tells me "keep it down."
I pay rent. A small hole
has opened in the backyard, a toothless mouth.
She tosses pennies in.
No man can fix this.

UNMAPPED SUBSIDENCE ZONES

*when they went to get their cows from the field for morning milking, all they discovered was
a large cave-in which had buried their animals.*[21]

When the man-car bumps the top of the shaft
a little bell rings. Ding! Like dogs, the men pile out —
a crew of identically-dressed mancar triplets,
formed from mud, rolled in ore and rust
with a hardhat stuck on to show which end goes up
and muddy boots glued to the bottom.
C'mon, ladies, git out! shouts the foreman,
Whatcha waiting for, a parasol?

While father and uncles march to the showers
I'm motionless, sitting in the mancar's last seat, numb,
floating above my body looking down at it, pitying
the sore hands on my sore lap, aching back.
I must slam into myself. I am waiting for it.
I dunno. I expected something more.

Rusty swore an oath to me, his refrain, in intimacy,
I'll turn to stone, he said, *if we ever call it quits*,
fine lexicon — & what did I hear each time he swore his oath?
I pictured some forlorn Laurentian outcrop,
Archean knuckle of greenstone worn by Lake Superior,
the rugged hump of Banded Iron behind his ma's house.
I'll turn to stone, he swore. Then didn't turn to stone,
only packed and turned and —

several floors below Negaunee, a low bell rang
as if someone was requesting service at the counter
of Salo's Meats, where the butcher lived upstairs.
That bell again, harder, impatient. *Service please!*

Anne Street's meadow rumbled, rumbled,
Helen Lahti's cows huddled at the center
like men in dark suits and white shirts
riding an Otis elevator, Down! down —
I'd like to say that safety gates banged shut between
the meadow and the town, a fence sprang up
to keep children from falling in, sneaking down to swim,
but that took decades, didn't it?

(((I'd like to say I rode the rumbling meadow down
with Helen's cows and drove them safely home
but I'm a coward you know—)))

Things were sinking, kept sinking.
Houses were relocated, bulldozed, pulled
from Snow Street, from Michigan; some left Negaunee Mine location,
heading east. Our cemetery was undermined — they shifted it.
In sum, said Reverend Kemppainen, *our very bones were moved.*

Mudge says: me & Muck
worked the Morris together, just a gate away
from Barnes-Hecker. That was a wet mine, I tell you what!
She ran down your collar the whole damn day and
dripped into your dreams as well.

Aili shows me a picture of her house, shifted gentle as a wool-swaddled infant,
says *when the men came to move our house out of the Caving Grounds, they promised
to be gentle, they said hey don't even bother — leave the pictures right there hanging
on the walls.* & Lila snorts, *ha! that wasn't how it worked at all, or maybe it was
different if you were the boss's wife, eh?* & Ernie says: *you seen our hole, right, old
Athens? She's dropping fast. Look for a roof the next time you're out there. That's the
Dry*[22] *where we changed our clothes, clean things in baskets, hung like drying onions.*

Roof's all you'll see of it now, whole thing's going down —

— no picnic, only a gray blanket
spread for lovers no longer in the meadow,
who were not drinking wine
nor looking deeply into each other's eyes;
under the maple, in unmowed grass,
a depression a deer might make, a trail of blood —
something wounded dragged through grass.
We do not wish to consider it, old tragedies,
wool and stains. Let the red, if we find it, be wine
spilled in passion. Don't forget there were lovers,
think of your young father
with an arm around your mother's slim waist, beaming and naïve.
Let the shirt-wrapped bundle hold their sandwiches,
slivered ham, ripe cheese, fragrant dark bread.
Nothing wrapped in a blue tarp teeming;
let nothing in our meadow hunger.

O the lichens have their work cut out for them
forgetting our names! & those worms waiting patiently
all in a row, our mourners — I've seen their heaved tunnels,
an iron-stained Night Shift of ghost worms in hardhats
arriving at the half-subsided mine gate, ghost worms
descending the steps into Athens Mine or
picking their way down to Jackson Pit, single file,
candles lighting the red scree — I don't
wish to follow this dark verse further
but will fulfill my duty, as the horse-drawn hearse
has a box to deliver, as the sexton has a hole to fill.

WHAT WAS DEPICTED IN MURALS AT THE DELFT?

Short of a compound fracture, they would not admit the shameful fact that one of their bones had broken — Finnish and Norse and Cornish bones are not supposed to break.[23]

To comprehend our town, you must climb peeled log ladders between Drift & Raise, horizon & pit, wasterock piles & tailing ponds big enough to see from space, unstable tunnels & forested friendly regions where sweaty deeds are ever-accompanied by hard liquor, steel implements, a bewildered Babel of cussing & hymns, impromptu roadside dumping, industrial fields atwinkle with shotgun-slivered amber. We saved our pennies for the matinee, the red-velvet curtains and popcorn. What was depicted in murals at the Delft? The artist captured us, our vivid *Apologia* deep-reach'd in scope complete with timelines of scientific discoveries: Seaborgium, pizza-parlor-cudighi effluvium, badly-dittoed violet-tinged maps depicting local townships, ownership plats, footnotes for serious scholars of rust, wood violets pressed between delicate psalms, bones shattered between slabs of *verfallene Schloesser*[24] — & delicately drawn in the foreground, a room of defunct newspapers printing stories in diverse languages, headlines announcing funerals & parades, illustrated sidebar advertisements for diamond-tip drills, Powders for Perfect Complexions, Cresco "cannot break at the waist" Corsets, patent remedies for flat-footedness & flat-chestedness, callus-reducing salves for working men, 10¢-a-day-rented Underwoods, elastic undergarments, self-massaging belts guaranteed to transform the bottom-heavy banker into a welter-weight contender, big-bellied mine bosses into vaudeville stars, Excess to Success! Magnets to reverse your Self-Centeredness! Cures for baldness, bee-sting, porcelain-stain, rust! *O Lordy yes! — & a purse-sized gun that shoots a lit cigarette if you press this hidden trigger, Bang!*

"AS THROUGH SOME VAST INSECURE CHEESE"

I thought of the 100s of uncomplaining iron miners a few miles away who daily plunged down into the chill and damp of ill-lit holes in the ground where for hours on end they groped their way about as through some vast insecure cheese.[25]

The soul descends, it prefers low places, mined-out locations,
Athens, Maas, Carp River marshes, folks struggling to make do —
Rilke said no matter how often he bent down he found God
& his God was dark as hematite-mud, a web
"made of a hundred roots
that drink in silence."

Quiet now men, take your seat, three abreast per plank
& weary. Tight fit. Ten rows deep, close enough to shave each other.
Filled, the mancar will send you down like a bobsled, then lift you again
from your drift, your duty in the shaft finished,
& swiftly. Keep your head down, Rusty!
Keep arms inside the car lest you lose a glove
at the wrist, lest you lose your pretty thoughts of poetry
or petty thoughts of vengeance to a blurry rockwall
cleaving black inches beyond your noggin.

Hematites' yearbook: "In case of nuclear war we might have to rely on primitive skills. It is encouraging to find out that 107 of us can cook a meal, 77 can read a compass and 28 are quite adept at hunting and fishing." The Miners First National Bank advertised "A good place to start saving!" Ah, but miners see deposits, think: how will I withdraw …

Give yourself to drift, a teacher advised me,
but he didn't mean Negaunee Mine, how it followed
the delineation of the orebody, and branching drifts

that followed money-rock — he meant a drifting current
of words, *don't fight your way upstream* — but didn't I —
didn't I mean to go the other way? Fine, anyway. I yield.
This drift knows more about me than me, Rusty says.
Let our boats be dragged along —

The worms form a muddy line,
little hematite miners ready for their shift.
The worms carry pails and tools, the worms wear workgloves.
The nightshift whistle blows and the worms advance.
The orebody shudders, anticipating their entry.

Meadow? Nope. Nobody's seen it lately.
You drained the sump?
You checked the dump?

I am alone onboard;
I ride the rattling meadow down! down,
suppressing a memory, swallowing a lump of —

Cecil the preacher from Republic who wanted to see first-hand
what it was like in the mine, since every man
in his congregation worked down there,
Rev. Cecil called up the bosses
pretending to be an engineering student
from Michigan Tech who'd driven down from Houghton
— O he got down there, sure enough, but he was a big guy,
got hung up in a tight space —
wedged in there, said it felt like forever before they got him unstuck,
the closest he ever wants to get to Hell.

They abandoned her, stopped pumping.
"Let her go" they said! Can you believe it?
Let groundwater have her back, they said.

⚒

So there's an engine left in the earth, *Cornish Pump*
tall as a three-story building, a tall-mast vessel
buried like a dark thought, a ship-in-a-bottle
of darkness and water, function finished.
Ground around here keeps shifting! —
"Michigan's on the move," the miners say, shrugging.
The roof of the stope
sinks to meet the floor, the breast sags
gravity-pressed, so much flesh
with no man's hands to urge her open;
the orebody closes like a steel-jawed trap
splintering subterranean timbers.

⚒

I tried my best, I begged and lied like Rev. Cecil
but three days after I missed my chance
trying to go down, my buddy Andy Jakela was
pretty near crushed to death. A swift collapse,
said he felt it all happening impossibly slow:
felt his legs break like kindling under the awful weight of iron
then his armbones breaking under stone,
heard them digging, shouting his name,
heard his own ribs cracking, one by one —

⚒

The Inspector of Mines defines "Caving Grounds" as areas where underground
mine shafts and tunnels "sometimes gave way." He writes it all in the past tense,
though he admits parts of town are still fenced off "because of the potential
danger from these *weakened areas*."

⚒

We blame the shafts, but after pit mining started, '70s,
the strength of blasting actually increased, our homes

rattled like bad teeth in rock-sockets coming loose.
You see the Senior float in our homecoming parade?

"Blow the top off the Hilltoppers!" urged the banner,
a Hematite Miner ready to plunge his detonator,

ready to blow away dozens of red dynamite lozenges
attached to the float with red crepe-paper streamers.

We laughed — he'll kill himself in the process!
Metaphors of labor leached into our language,

seeped into our water table; it is a hard, hard water
and we swig it like whiskey from the tap.

The deep-shaft mines were shuttering,
subsiding, when the Hematites Class of '63
painted their class motto on fresh plaster,
that mural where we enter town under a railroad trestle:
"So Much To Build From This Foundation!"
Proudly painted. Such optimism. It lasted a year
before the trestle plaster cracked
revealing red-banded jasper —

A FIELD OF MUDSWALLOWS

Once upon a time, a miner undermined this town
until his own home slowly sank into the basement floor
and further: Down! down, into the caving ground.

On Snow Street, gardens grew unstable and playgrounds
gave way beneath their teeter-totters. Today, rusting signs warn
DANGER : KEEP OUT. By danger, we mean "Caving Ground"

— just an empty, ordinary-looking meadow now,
just a field of mudswallows and sumac and buckled cement porches
where (*Once upon a time*) a miner undermined his own hometown

like a nutworm, moving from the heart-out, tearing down
wide hematite columns for their ore, the underground supports
that were a sort of spine, deep down, bracing up the Caving Grounds.

Once upon a time, a miner removed his own spine; it sounds
absurd unless you've seen the earth swallow yards, flagpoles, front doors.
This is no fairy tale: The Miner Who Undermined His Own Hometown

— it was his job. So his lawn dropped several feet; his house was zoned "unsound"
and the foundation razed. Perhaps there's no redeeming moral to the story
of how, in recent times, a miner undermined this town.

Perhaps we drop without a solid reason: *Down! down,*
into the Caving Grounds.

RUSTY — DON'T PUT IT PAST HIM

A long time ago a man discovered that he could make an impressive sound by dragging a large piece of iron through a field of stones.[26]

Rusty — don't put it past him. He'd do anything on half a dare and deny it with an altarboy's eyes while you pulled his thumbnail out. One time, Rusty's down at the harbor and whassisface, that fisherman with a place on the point, you know who I'm talking about, he's getting ready to make a haul of fresh fish to Munising — summer tourists, they go through lake trout like nobody's business. So the old fart sees Rusty looking hung over, tells him to jump in, keep him company. The two of em put out — Rusty's soaking up sun, sees a bunch of tarps and crawls over to sleep out of the wind. Wakes up a couple hours later and thinks he's died, bones so cold and stiff he can't hardly move arms or legs, circulation all numb underneath, and his upturned face red as a fire hydrant. *S-s-s-s-s-so b-b-b-b-blue my back was damn near frost-bit*, Rusty tells it later. The story always gets him a free drink when he tells somebody new — how he fell asleep on a load of block ice, sunburnt on top, and frostbit below — the ice keeping those fish fresh for tenner-a-tail dinners!

A FULL-COLOR MAP OF THE LOCAL TERRAIN

Then go down into the dense damp darkness of the mine with shovels and picks. Here his only light, for the next 10 hours, will be 2 candles worn one at a time on his hat. Later a carbide lamp would be used to give more light. I'm sure the candles blew out with every breeze and movement of air.[27]

Arbutus recalls the scene,
four miles her grandfather walked to work & back
bookending the unmarked miles spent underground,
ten hours of burning labor, two tallow candles
worn on the hat. Exhausting day
& four miles still waited heading home.
Her dad, the miner's son, fared no better
— when his hands were bloody from shoveling
the mine boss shrugged, said sure boy, you shovel
your 10 tons today & everyday
or somebody else holds your shovel tomorrow

I tell them right straight,
put your money into educating
your family instead of drinking and cigarettes
save as much of your money as you can.[28]

Was he ever melancholy? Hell yes,
saved everything: rubber-bands, matchbooks,
odd bits of string   made do
     did it himself & if he sings
he sings of you, Negaunee, his father
shooting his mother before suicide
in the Land of Milk and Honey   bacon-trees
potato-and-blood-sausage mirages
— men of his generation learned to never count on plenty.
The Depression was an empty stope
inside him, always.

     ⚒

(2 men climbing an electrical pole in harnesses)

O see *"the ease and comfort Reddy Kilowatt, our electric*
servant, brings to every home in this age of Electrical Lighting!"

The sorting ladies down at St. Vinnie's
— they keep an eye out for me,
set aside mugs and plates and platters
from their donation bins
whatever arrives broken, missing handles, roughly handled —
they know how I love what's shattered;
they know on rainy days I'm apt to sit
on my screenporch with a box of cracked
tureens and crockery fashioning scenes:
Jesus Meeting the Anishinaabe, Mineral Exploration, Goose Clan,
Old Growth Hemlocks, stories with a bit of everything
tossed in, kitchen sinks, burnt moose bones,
Diverse Bits glued and grouted together,
until it seems Shattered Matter is a single, comprehensive vessel,
our local narrative, our holy pastiche —

The Inspector of Mines? — he's reading De Re Metallica: "*If a shaft is very deep
and no tunnel reaches to it … or when a tunnel is of great length and no shaft reaches
to it, then the air does not replenish itself … there is, therefore, a necessity for machines
which the Greeks call pneumatikai and the Latins spiritales — though they do not
give forth any sound — which enable the miners to breathe easily and carry on their
work.*"

Have you read the stone tablet
                    which some say is ancient and true
                            and others call a hoax
found under the roots of an old-growth pine
& those who believe the thing is real
swear they've translated it — *Ogam!*
They say Phoenicians came for our copper,
tree roots the most vital detail

for trees grow over
& obscure   — pound a nail,
tie a strand of barbed wire around the trunk
and it swells over girdling as it grows
cementing Other into itself
                    ((concentric rings))
narrative grown into a Larger Text.

⚒

Why do you persist in your doubt?
there is nothing new under the sun, says Rusty.
In our general vicinity have been found
slabs of float copper the size of dolphins,
iron so pure it could be forged, fresh from earth;
a series of berms and mounds which form,
in a hardwood forest, the outline of a whale.
Inside these earthworks: *charcoal*
suggesting a dual purpose in some lost ritual,
alchemical fuel for primitive metal forges,
a device for diverting the wind into the
mouth of fire, mouth of the mineshaft.

⚒

Collapse? The policeman refers you to Leo LaFonde.
Leo LaFonde says *t-t-t-t-alk to Reverend Rudy*.
Rudy says call the Inspector of Mines,
he checks the fences, caps, shafts, he'd know
that soft spot you're worried about.

⚒

Call Tiresias[29], tell him to dig a new trench.
The abandoned mines are angry, their mouths are opening,
old gods down there, rusty spirits with smashed altars
and names we've forgotten, they're hungry —
I'm not yet fluent in their tongue but I believe, yes,
they're demanding a *sacrifice*.

36

⚒

To fill the hours while my bones mend
my sister sent a picture puzzle which promises,
when completed, to be
Spiritus: A Full-Color Map of the Local Terrain!
denoting every town on the Iron Range
with historical illustrations, ornate call-outs,
annual tonnage, relevant saints and scriptural passages,
names of founding businesses down both sides
and hammer-&-pick symbols marking myriad shafts,
subsidence zones, great open pits, railroads that hauled away
our Place. Each night I labor over detonated
fragments trying at last to fit together what has never
fit together.

IF IT CAN'T BE GROWN, IT'S GOTTA BE MINED

There's a miner inside you, drilling,
setting charges, trying to dislodge your heart,
— *she's a hard bitch but she'll assay okay, blue iron*
he brags at the Venice, the Crow Bar, J.T.'s Shaft,
says he's found something rare in you, glittery steel,
only you don't know anything about him yet,
your inner miner in a yellowed undershirt
and bad teeth; he limps out of your sleeping mouth
each morning with a yawn, ore-stained man
exhausted by the night shift, leaving his drift.
He works hard, drinks too much beer and
says he's growing a pot-belly like a pumpkin,
thumps himself one-handed, his belly drum,
sings along with the radio when he thinks you're sleeping,
off-key, says *sure, ya betcha, alrighty den fine, da hell wit' you!*

He mutters to himself — deep inside you.
Bumper sticker: *If it can't be grown, it's gotta be mined.*
Says he worries about folks like you —
'dem as lack the brains God gave da goose.
Hairs thick as gray moss inside his nostrils.
Stoop to my level! he shouts, standing
on your sleeping tongue with a finger raised;
calls the mines his "local girls" — says he's
had his way with every one of them,
never finished school and wants you to know
he's sixty-five now, bachelor, never read a poem his whole life
and he's proud of that too, *lest you count dirty lim'ricks, eh!*

> *He's got six big ideas. Five don't work.*
> *Right now he's repeating them to you.*[30]

Says he wouldn't object to sleeping with you someday
if you ever met him halfway, if you wore a dress
& shaved your legs, acted willing,
if you ever caved —

HE DID NOT DIG DEEPER FOR FEAR OF DISAPPOINTMENT

Surely and rapidly the great and aged men, who in their prime entered the wilderness and claimed the virgin soil as their heritage, are passing to their graves ...[31]

O sure, I've got a picture somewhere of the big cave-in. Back in the thirties, that one, you know, 'fore my time, and I'm 73. That was the biggest, not the last — there were others. They didn't take down our houses and fence it all off for many years.

To his wife, he calls "Hey Mrs. J., remember that time we were snowmobiling down there — there was that big hole had opened up in the street? Was it Iron? Middle of the night, we're calling up the Company telling 'em to send somebody down there right away."

"No, it was Park," she yells back, "when we lived down on the far end."

Too many holes to keep straight, he says.

⚒

"If we're talking holes, of course, there's Cliff, right there under downtown Ishpeming." He finds a dim photo, says "this isn't too old, see how his helmet's got a modern light on it, he's operating the scraper?" Beyond the miner, flash revealed a rough wall and a crush pile below his boots. Beyond that — nothing. Blackness swallowed the light without yielding further details. "Now that was hard ore, they say it won't cave the way Negaunee caved. But yer hole under Ishpeming, yer mine got opened up down there, connecting everything, all the levels grew together, so wide a guy couldn't see the other side, so high he couldn't see the ceiling."

A man couldn't see the other side of the stope he worked? "Too far," Rollie insists. Too dark, too high. "One guy I know worked that stope with his son until they closed the mine. Before him, his father worked the same orebody, his grandfather too I suppose —picture the size of that hole they made down there, generation after generation, right under downtown. If it ever caved, I guess our whole town'd go down. They say it won't, the Company! But it sure gives you pause."

Back when I was living in Cornish Town with my kids, that's when a kid drowned in the pit, open shaft at the bottom of a swimming hole, a pit filled with water. I was out with my neighbor fishing that afternoon, and my girls was over t'his house, playing with his kids. We come back over the hill, and see trucks and the people all over; somebody says, "yeah, a kid drowned in the flooded shaft of the Jackson Pit." And my heart just stopped beating right then and there. "Boy or girl?" They didn't even know yet; nobody knew. I dunno, we started running to the house where our kids were. The boy who drowned, he must have been eleven. I wish I had that boy's photo now.

Let me show you this: between Negaunee and Palmer, that's where I was born. (He shows a small photograph, pointing with a blackened fingernail). *Bellevue.* Now that was a beautiful farm, you see that barn? Just huge, my lord! Built in a great X, the center was like a cathedral inside! In the distance, you see the dots? Dipping tanks. The farm raised sheep and potatoes and vegetables for the Company. Most beautiful farm you ever saw! When the mine stopped using the barn for sheep, they turned it into four houses — four families lived there. We lived there, we raised potatoes and vegetables in the Big Field, but the mine owned our land, the mine took our crops. Now, let me tell you one more thing about my home: *that whole area is buried under a mountain of wasterock now* — maybe the Big Field is still there, a bit of it. A bit was visible last I checked, but that must be ten years or more, that stockpile keeps growing, the rocks keep sliding down, so odds are against it. The Big Field was beautiful. Grew potatoes you wouldn't believe. Big Field's gone forever now, buried, I guess.

Geno said, "Show me a landscape where they suffered like we did. *Pompeii?* Okay, maybe Pompeii, eh? Ash. But that mountain blew apart like a storm, it took everyone in a single night, praise God, it buried 'em quickly."

That tramp who'd been living all winter in the Caving Grounds told everyone his name was Cacus. Said his father died in a mine fire. Later, Carnegie's librarian Ms. Olson said *Cacus — wasn't that Vulcan's son? didn't he live in a cave under his father's mountain?*

At the Mine Workers' Appreciation Day
our local Representative spoke: "Every day at noon
when the (mine) blasts it shakes a little plaster down from my house …"[32]
The whole crowd chuckled knowingly. *Ha! Elect him again!*
Hell, who hasn't felt their world shudder every time a blast detonated;
who hasn't patted their wallet t'remind himself
what he's getting outa t'deal? If yer house, yer garden,
yer neighborhood must be blasted to rubble and debris
it's fine to be bribed along the way!

Bodies exhumed from tephra show we lingered longer
than needed. What's your nostalgia for old meadows worth at the market, Eino?
Can you buy bread with it? What's your daughter's cedar hope chest filled with,
mother to daughter, empty except our finely-knitted knack
for missing what we lost at birth, or never even had!

Take my word for it, says Rusty, our legacy lies in extracting
what we were given, inexhaustible stands of *towering virgin timber*[33],
them green girls, grandpa said he had his way with all of them.
I've seen Empire's red dust blazing up like all our land was set afire,
a funeral pyre. For a while, guide books called Empire's rockpiles "*the highest
     point in Michigan!*" — but it was a man-made erection, unnatural.
(((A correction was made in subsequent printings.)))

We are skilled at embroidery:

> *The first rodents were stowaways in the large bags of grain brought into the mine … their*
> *offspring, born into the blackness of the mine, were blind, vicious, and grew to be as large as*
> *cats. Because their only food was the large timbers and cedar lagging, they developed front*
> *teeth as large as beavers.*[34]

Vicious earth out by Rolling Mill location, too,
Rollie gestures to his wife. *Tell her about your school bus.*

O, that, well, she says (((she was a kid)))
out between Negaunee and Rolling Mill location
when the school bus picked us up and brought us around the hill.

Somebody's miner-father admitted the land
was all undermined & couldn't be trusted
with the weight of a yellow school bus.
Suddenly it wasn't allowed — the county painted
a line on the road the bus couldn't drive over. I looked for it,
but it's invisible now, that line that couldn't be crossed.

Home. We walked down the rest of our hollowed road from then on.
I said, wait — you walked over Caving Grounds?
We crossed it morning & night, hell, we lived here, she said.
We were kids. We were light.

It is instructive to view abandoned mines as subterranean
cathedrals, the Great Stope sacred to Vulcan and his boy Cacus,
that bicep-and-blasting-cap-chiseled chamber
whose golden back-pulsing ceiling dome rises 200' above the floor
rivaling in dimension the Hagia Sophia —

If only I can figure out what that Thing is
out there on the horizon — *the Future, where we all want to be*
— if only I can make pilgrimage to it, and kneel there,
drink that holy water flowing cold and ferrous from the pipe, then
I can align myself & all of us, wherever we stand, like magnetic particles,
can move a common goal to that hidden pole. Tomorrow!

Under thin topsoil, under tree roots, under snow,
a compass is often useless in this region where
north is wherever you turn, a magnetic landscape
tugging the tip of your tiny arrow to her ruddy bosom
saying *here my love — further west, a bit south!*
further east, yes, here, here, O here!

⚒

Each week, one candle in the candlestick is extinguished, removed. They practice self-flagellation — vying to be nailed to wooden crosses, hung from great nails through palms and feet, lifted, ceremonially processed as others walk along whipping their backs bloody with bolt-studded strops. The Church banned *Penitentes*, of course, but cannot end the underground sect.

⚒

I have told no one but you of that night I slept in Caving Grounds —
the Section 16 Mine: a garden of bone-white snapped snags,
shattered piles of blue iron, sun-warmed, glinting, ruins
where great worms seem to have surfaced,
raising piles of specularite around their holes.
I meant to sleep between twin
pits of black water, made my bed on a mossy land-bridge
of ferrous rock. But upon this same bridge, beast-headed gods
strode back and forth all night, cawing and howling,
— how easily they moved despite their creaking age!
They walked with neither canes nor torches,
passing over that black bridge where I lay
terrified, flanked by flooded pits shimmering on each side
and lit from above by the light of a billion stars.

> *"We thought it would be important to remind everyone about the young people who died in the shafts, because nobody really knows about it," senior Ross Montcalm said. "We want to show that in order to make Negaunee what it is today,* sacrifices were made. *"*[35]

Every season or so, we say *the gods demand sacrifices.*

The Company reports this.

Which gods, specifically, asks Rusty,
Who among us heard their requests?

OLSON BROS. WASTE MANAGEMENT

Joke was they managed the waste by merely sorting
junk by type: fridges-stoves this pile, sofas-chairs that,

glass-cans-windows-barrels, a billion parts nobody'd take for scrap,
— o, but their genius was in knowing this land like the back

of their hand, unmarked shafts the hidden piggybanks where anything
they dropped stayed down, *abracadabra*. Ka-ching! You'd do the same —

myriad Empire boys sent away for magic coins, rings, brochures,
kits that promised to impart the Art of Making Stuff Disappear!

You'd start small at first, sure: a few bright coins behind your ear,
silk scarves, cards, bags of wormy crab-apples, hardened house paint,

working your way up to shingles, beds, tarp-shrouded loads,
hell, some old widower nobody'd miss, *there's bottomless holes*

Paavo swore drinking brandy, *if you just know where to look*
and his brother kicked him hard under the bar. *We're Waste Professionals,*

said Ole, his soft hands folded smoothly as a funeral director's,
perfect nails. *It's magic, boys. We wave our wands, make shit go Poof.*

III.

What we conceal
Is always more than what we dare confide.[36]

Barnes-Hecker was sealed, and the area is now a quiet lake on which surviving relatives still toss floral wreathes in memory of those 1,000 feet below the surface.[37]

Jos viina terva ja sauna ei auttaa kuolema on tosi.[38]

And house by house their walls cave in.[39]

COME SUNDAY, THE DOG OF HIS THOUGHTS WILL BURY
SOMETHING UNSPEAKABLE IN YOUR MUDDY GARDEN

Dearest Christ,
how's the new job coming
— administrative assistant, you said?
did my last postcard mention how the tulips
are poking up their ruddy erections from
every corner of the yard? so many, I forgot
the humus held so many! though it's too soon
for bloom — cruel spring — remember the rose
which should have graced my back gate eternally,
"Paul's Ever-blooming Scarlet, winter-hardy to zone 3"
— the one I mail-ordered from Gurney's? It froze.
But then a seed catalogue is a list of the deceased
and not a bible. (Or a bible too, you think?)

Bless me, but I get confused.

ANOTHER THING ABOUT RUSTY IS HOW HE NEVER LEARNS

Let's go to Isle Royale, Rusty says to me one night — I'd had more'n a few and the bar was closing so I say *Hell, I'm in! Big Bay to Isle Royale in an outboard in the middle of the night* — I know what you're thinking, right? But it was balmy, the stars were searchlights for a Hollywood movie, and the Lake was sleepy-creepy-smooth-as-glass, plus we were well in the bag, which helped us decide. An hour or two out, I'm tired of sipping Rusty's crappy whiskey and I says to him, *give me one of my beers*, and he lobs me a cold bottle. *An opener too* — and Rusty says *hell, I don't keep no openers on my boat, she's a whiskey boat*, and I says *no problem, throw me yer pliers or a wrench or screwdriver whatever* and after a minute Rusty says, *no toolbox*. No toolbox? My brain goes numb then. I'm looking at the Keweenaw lights blinking "come-come-come" and the Huron Island light, spinning "dumb-dumb-dumb" and I see, finally, how small we are, and dumb. How icy and unplumbed this Lake, with northern lights staining her lip green. *Rusty*, I says, *turn yer boat around goddammit, we're not drunk enough to die tonight, Rusty.*

AFTER IRON'S BOOM GOES BUST

No industry in this port town's future, only tourism
based on a memory of industry, and relics for sale
including postcards no one sends, craft beers named
for mines, smoked fish, pine slivers, iron pellets in baggies.
I captain the oreboat, Paavo B. Tiresias, paid to stay
just out of sight, anchored nightly behind the island
— not a bad job. The lift bridge makes
a special show of lifting for us; appreciative crowds
turn out with their cameras. Down at the oredocks,
taconite spouts slip into place with grease and wires,
a rehearsed ease. The rumbling of the ore as it enters
is pre-recorded audio. Red dust lifting in the wind billows
from the deck where we've sprinkled it, each morning.
After iron's boom goes bust we extract Trust.
Bilge and ballast adjust automatically to make the
freighter ride low, leaving harbor. Faux smoke seems.
Cardboard crew. A tugboat just for show, helpful.
Leaving, I sound the ship's foghorn— kids love it.

THE BARNES-HECKER MINE DISASTER AS A SCHRÖDINGER'S BOX

we could not know which was the case, so there was no choice, scientifically, but to regard the cat as 100% alive and 100% dead at the same time.[40]

Gravedigger of girlhood: whose barn-cats lie along the granary wall?
Who brings their loving bones a bowl of milk & for whom do they purr?
Their doting girl is grown & gone. No rough tongue, no phone can reach her
     now

who gravely scratched each name in barn wood before the granary was
repainted. *Who remembers?* Maybe future archaeologists will exhume
her furred dead, curled in holes as if curled in sunlight still. Hardest knowing

she shoveled the sand over fur, buried too a bowl of milk, dandelions.
But — air holes? Did Schrödinger's atom decay? There is uncertainty.
The cat dies either way but remains alive so long as we do not know.

Certainly we know our worst local tragedy was the Barnes-Hecker,
every miner buried where he stood, shovel-in-hand, or swept down-shaft by mud,
only one clawed his way to the surface, poor Rutherford, who told what he knew

of the tomb, of mud, of every level filled in fifteen minutes a thousand feet deep.
The mine proved too unstable for rescue: abandoned & capped,
51 names in stone & a comfort to say *they all died instantly, you know.*

Only — I was given a story in confidence, gravedigger. Must you really know?
How one was sealed in a seeping engine room at the bottom of the filling shaft
with a phone line to the engine house on the surface, still working. O terrible
     knowing,

how he wept for an hour & begged to tell his wife goodbye & they cut the line.
Then it was over, & over quickly we assume, though nothing was exhumed
so we may equally believe he lives with Schrödinger's cat on his lap, still purring.

MISS IRON RANGE SINGS REBA

How you done me wrong,
Baby crank it up!
Until you blow the speakers out your Chevy truck.[41]

Come Sunday, Rusty, we'll stroll
along the Caving Grounds fenceline
down to Rautamäki Senior Center,
grab ourselves empty folding chairs
— you saving this for anybody? No?
It's a creaky end to wondering at last
who'll win the local talent contest;
who'll be named *least likely to escape*
this collapsing town's gravitational field,
who'll be crowned Miss Iron Range:
most likely not your favorite niece
the one with straight As, braced teeth
and a job at the library; more likely
your neighbor's feral grandchild,
that blonde girl rough as beachgrass
wasting her summer swatting fish-flies,
oiling herself on lakeshore sand
in earshot of the ore dock's rumbling
freighters and sooty coal yard,
a pre-melanoma case whose special talent
is brazen flirting, opening zippers with her lips
and lip-syncing along with the radio —
now she sings Reba, singing loud, singing flat,
and when she blows the words she just laughs
like she's not on stage, like she's flying
down the road with her hair out the window
spit-polishing dust from her tin tiara,
flip-flops propped on a new boy's pickup
dash, her toenails painted black.

EPISTLE OF ART MAKI

Hope this finds you good
Ma sat me down & made me write you
'fore she'd give me more cinnamon Trenary toast
Your cousins come to camp last week, cut brush

& clean things. Couple 6-packs of Black-Label
they got carried away with trimming those red pines
you planted in a double row between the sauna & lake.
What were you, 1st grade? Arbor Day, your teacher

sent you home w/seedlings. I got used to them red pines
some privacy for a body coming out of the sauna
like a plate of steamed redskin potatoes, getting up nerve
to jump off the dock. Drunk dumbasses

they cut all the little limbs off, made me mad!
Unnatural. When you coming home, Rusty?
Always more work than I can keep up with fixing
Grandpa's camp, roof shingles all gone to moss,

screens shot, window frames need reglazing before
the panes fall plumb out & that red handpump in the kitchen —
pump all you want but water don't lift to the surface anymore.
But I don't think it's the leathers, Rusty.

I think something's wrong here (pointing). Down below.

COME SUNDAY, RUSTY, LET US SEEK THE HYPOGEUM

Let us descend to make our cold-sweat offerings in an old stope
larger than the world's only prehistoric underground temple
Hypogeum of al-Saflieni of Malta
comparing it with our own ferrous church,
Iron Mtn., a man-hollowed district sacred to Vulcan
where Rusty entered often with a friend — *it was our thing*
he says, of trespassing in the under
world, mine-creeping
down chutes & ladders, slipping into nameless drifts
abandoned cross-cuts
until that final night they found themselves
descending into the Big Stope:
soooo vaaaast! Rusty says, as if held vowels
sum his remembering,
how flashlight beams barely brushed the far walls,
a bat-pulsing roof-dome carved by sheared rock slabs
dropping, dripping, an open shaft below the stope
deep enough to contain the Empire State Bldg.
further, no bottom visible, grandfather-mined,
wooden ladder rungs sagging mushroom-slick
beneath, his friend growing hysterical:
why we still going down, Rusty?
why we doing this?
& Rusty says he saw he didn't know, himself,
couldn't say & a rotten rung cracked
& he climbed up, and that was the last time
he went down

enough is enough, swears Rusty, cross
my heart, I'm over all that. Ashes to ashes
rust to rust, we probed them father-wounds
with our fingers — let us kneel and leave! Hell,
we seen what needed seeing.

GRYPANIA SPIRALIS

Between Palmer and Negaunee, the orebody descends
& machines gouge deeper to follow it into
down-plunging sedimentary layers — *hematite, ferrous chert,*
magnetite. I dated a fellow who called all the layers *taconite*
but that was crude, I felt. Taconite was an industrial process,
not orebody but *beneficiated product*, blended, kilned pellets,
so different from the torn-flesh terraces of red-gray shimmer!
Two great pits of marbled flank steak, gash-lush,
a stone wall left between for a switchbacked haul-road,
zig-zagging suture scars, vistas into epic terrain.
In the cathedral of Empire Mine we are fly specks on a psalm page,
dust motes wafting through a vast sunlit transept.

At a certain depth, geologist Tsu-Ming Han
found something holy: a thin strata of ore, easily separated.
He peered inside as we'd turn pages in a book
and there it was, written in the alphabet of *Grypania spiralis*,
the oldest visible-to-the-naked-eye fossil[42] in the world,
all Cs and Js and Os, squirmings of ancient sea life preserved:
the oxygen they exhaled became our atmosphere,
catalyst for ferric precipitation, iron drawn from ancient seas
deposited in red-mud bottom layers to become Empire.
Precambrian. Ore-origin. Evolutionary evidence.
Yet the pit must grow larger, the Company warned.
The wall will be mined out, the book of fossils pulped,
no line, no sacred text bars Empire from profit.

Tsu Ming opens sheets of broken ore in his hands —
shows me the pages. *It is a poem*, I say,
but he says *no, this is Genesis, life's brittle book*
& we gasp as we pry it further open, seeing for ourselves
what is written, rushing to fill our bags and pockets,
commanded to save whatever we can.

HOW THE ABANDONED LANDS SPEAK

Jane I left you and them boys for no other reason than this ... to procure a littl property by the swet of my brow so that we could have a place of our own that I might not be a dog for other people any longer.[43]

Moses, descending the mountain, returned with stones — the Old Law. This is the New Law: finding an historic mine site, high up the ridge,

disturb nothing.

⛏

Reaching the first blank page of your sketchbook, record an outline of the deflated cabin, the yawn of the shaft mouth barred only by beamlitter where the leaning headframe, a working man's Pisa, recently toppled on the hole. Survey in silence what remains — silence, as we learned to pray. Selecting a section of earth, ask yourself some sort of question that cannot be answered in the spin of an hour: what can we learn, for example, by inspecting the details of failure?

⛏

Adherence to the New Law does not guarantee success. The shaft does not go down too far — just far enough so the air, sinking, uncirculating for years, has gone bad: soured of monoxide, pocketing itself along a drift as so many bitter worms cocoon their metamorphing forms to stone. It's a shallow hole, a short drift. And fatal. Haven't you ever believed — for a few weeks, at least? — that a life of honest working would pay off? Privately, each tongue knows the good, salty taste of our own sweat, the metallic honey of blood, that throbbing knuckle we dumbly hammered open then sucked to staunch the flow? Although it's also true we lost the vein, digging, or maybe the ore never assayed as richly as we hoped — to sell the failed venture, we might have to salt the mine, using a shotgun to fire real gold dust, impregnating the poor walls with shimmer, a false promise visible to anyone who might buy ...

Admit it. Under the Old Law, how many lies did we profit by?

⛏

Note, on your hand-drawn map, the precise location of foundations, tools, clutter — later, what appeared to be trash may speak to you in the old language of purpose. The coffee-can with a wire stitched through one side? The wire was a makeshift handle; the can held a candle, protecting the flame as it limpingly projected its little glow forward, a poorman's lantern — a shadowgee. Or that cluster of rusting junk turns out to be *Mill-in-a-Box*, never assembled, mail-ordered from a 1912 Mill & Smelter Catalogue: cogwheel, grinder and crusher still resting on their rotten wood palettes — each cast-iron component packed up this mountainside by mule or the back of a man. (If there are mulebones nearby, you may know for sure.) And if it's not too much like poetry, describe in the margin how this machinery forms a circle in the clearing, a ring of rusty skulls arranged as if for ceremony — in the middle, you assume, something was about to be assembled, something that would roar when it speaks.

In the Abandoned Lands.
Soon.

⚒

If you are the sort who needs reminders, something tangible to hold onto like a Post-it Note or a string around your finger, something for later, select a most ordinary-looking rock, a bit of schist chipped free by pick-ax or blasted loose from within the shaft, mucked out, hoisted to the surface — the hard stuff of dreams. Hard to tell now, looking at your dry old rock, but maybe in a fairy tale it fed a man, maybe someone wrung a few nights' nourishment from it, or tried to anyway, in a bible story — a shard of verse from the Book of Hope, that silvery firewater flecked with glints of fools-gold.

⚒

Under the Old Law, the world was a bargain. If you examine sepia photographs with a microscope, you notice tiny price tags tied to boulders and dangling from the lowest branch of every pine: 1¢, 3 cents, etc. Sales clerks, unfortunately, were hard to locate — a hundred miles or more from your mineral claim, from the drift that needed timbering to keep a roof from falling in.

To accommodate, most American Landscapes used the honor system: take what you want now & pay in the box provided. A man's word was golden: *On my honor! On my mother's grave!*

Soon the terrain was shorn, stumped, pitted, exhausted. It was inefficient.

And yet convenient — we all agreed.

⚒

"*What went on underground,*" archeologists of the New Law preach, "*can be determined by what's left aboveground.*"

To prove this, they hike the hills by day doing no harm, inventing a history of what happened here until it mule-trains together into meaning: impossible slopes, rusted boilers, human capacity for hope, tailings and open shafts. Descending, chests fired to bursting under a heavy tablet of all they've seen, archeologists send postcards to lovers inexplicably left behind & vice versa. None have yet discovered those skeletons far below the western ledge, eleven mules strung together in death by the stagger-load they carried in life: a continuous length of heavy-gauge cable coiled from beast-of-burden to beast-of-burden, a silver hoist-rope whose echo lingers: we have burdens in common.

Each night, returning like miners without dirty nails, archaeologists study the local tavern where a jukebox blares "*a man ain't made of stone, a man ain't made of steel.*" Let them rock themselves to sleep with shots of Goldschläger and bits of glittering bedtime stories overheard between men of calluses, dredging the tailings of their own lives. Well maybe, we admit, there's some Truth there, buried under the whiskey.

⚒

Who's been down there, lately? Who's to say there isn't something wild or holy, maybe even a hermit living in the high, abandoned mines? In ancient times, wasn't every exhalation from the earth considered oracular?

Who's down there? the archeologist called, suddenly frightened. The shaft walls were constricting under pressure, splintering great timbers.

Nobody's down here, a voice from below answered. Nobody.

And a mudswallow flew out.

⚒

Everywhere your finger touches the map, you are Other, academic tourist, stranger. Nobody talks to strangers anymore. Nobody builds living birds from mud.

Be satisfied with your own thoughts, muttering above the treeline — remote, hell yes, but someone with better aim was here already, putting the lame shaft houses out of their misery, making holes for the light, helping whiskey bottles seed their shards among the weeds — some hint why sunsets are so brilliant at this altitude, despite the narrow old path, drifts that never panned out, the bones of that sweetly stubborn little mule, Hope.

How we stumble, bray, drunk on an Optimism of such high proof it blinds us.

REOPENING THE CAVING GROUNDS

Where shade trees lean together guarding
fenced boundaries, blazed with rusted *danger signs*
new plastic placards offer LOTS FOR SALE
the realtor's selling cheap, another fortune to be made
on the land's twisted back, no questions asked.

Past midnight, I hear the sound of the gates opening
at last, the Caving Grounds, re-opening!
Some Being squats there holding a skeleton key,
rusty hinges squealing, a rat with his tail
crushed under an orecar.

No mineral rights. No wound-probing please.
Imagine your dream home here, build to suit,
hematite-strewn earth still soft as a puffball smoking
underfoot, voids colonizing voids, releasing dark
silky spore-clouds, lack lusting after lack.

From this dream, no amount of shaking escapes,
the screaming of the iron gates awakens & yet I am
not awake — it repeats & I am still not awake!
Who forged the key? & what beast turns it?
Who will be invited to return, at what price?

IV.

Tis all in peeces, all cohaerence gone.[44]

imagine taking a piece of iron, for instance, and chopping it in half, then chopping one of those pieces in half, and so on. Could you keep this up indefinitely? Democritos believed you could not — you would eventually have the smallest possible piece of iron, and he called this an atom.[45]

miners from Negaunee's Jackson Mine plainly assumed they were squarely at the center of their universe; everything flowed and revolved around and about this pulsing central core.[46]

The pebble hunters didn't know that there was a little hole in the sock. As the two friends walked along, their pebbles dropped out through the hole ...[47]

CERTAIN VEINS REMAIN GUARDED

I don't want to sing this anymore!
My heart has a verse to deliver, but I am weary of delivering it,
weary of moss, rusty skips, rotten boards over holes.

⚒

Yet the Great Lakes roar!
The night sky a sea where phosphorescent minnows veer,
spelling alien symbols against their black slate depths.

⚒

Find a Subject worthy of your inward circling,
as a dervish circles one thing for endless hours or decades,
turning around a column, a single point.
I imagine myself in the shaft, calcified whorling rooms
of the snail's columella — pump engine gone but a massive wheel
still spinning from the energy of my *paying-attention,*
my scrawling, looping, ecstatic pen.

⚒

Certain veins remain *guarded.* This is right.
There is a silver so pure it burns the eyes of any who glimpse,
an iron reserved for the Master of the Forge, copper ore so holy
I may not mention it by name —

⚒

Rusty says he'll check his calendar and get back to me.
Sure, I say. If it was so easy, revealing ourselves to each other utterly,
there would be nobody at the taverns on Friday night,
looking around, spinning hopefully.

MIRACLE IN THE MUSEUM OF IRON INDUSTRY

With a little imagination you can see people all over America mining, processing, smelting, refining, carrying, fabricating, and finally assembling the component parts to make an automobile ...[48]

About rusting they were never wrong,
our deep-shaft miners: how well they knew
the holy mystery of oxidization; how it must take place
in the permanent exhibition's swarm of long-beaked pick-axes
preserved like feeding mosquitoes, rust corroding each iron proboscis
(*only the Curator doesn't know*) where it pierces the faux-rock wall;
or the crowbar rusting in the mannequin's tireless grip, prying
more imaginary ore from the roof of the humid, recreated drift
— how, even as our own devout mothers idle in the stormy
confessional of the Brushless-Touchless Car Wash
as the rocker-washer regathers its dripping bowels for a final
underbody pass of Rust Inhibitor — how even then
there must always be a boy reinventing the wheel, a girl feeding
nails to a chirping nest of open-mouthed jars, each crucible
translucent, half-filled with kerosene, vinegar, Diet Pepsi,
Palmolive, milk, urine — *she'll never lose her love for cooking, that girl*
but few will understand her search for God: Rust, the Secret Recipe by which
one substance alchemically becomes another, that dreadful Rorschach
she saw once, in *A Child's Big Book of Bible Stories, Illustrated* —
the Stranger's secret identity revealed by his hands, palms up: red holes
eternally unhealed. For every father buying Rustoleum,
for every martyr with his finger in the dam,
there's a girl like her, with her pocketknife in the family's rusting fender,
widening the wound — *for Curiosity? for chrisssake!*

Catching iron flakes in the cup of her upraised palm.
Even in Brueghel's painting of Icarus: how well we ignored the Descent itself,
as if the child would merely drop into an entry-level position in the mines.
Beneath the flaking pigment, x-rays of Icarus reveal an earlier failure:
Still Life with Hard Hat, some fatally-dented relic from the fall.
Otherwise, the paintings are the same: undulating sea, umber field,
the distant oredocks, the gaunt, omniscient eagle with a fishhook rusting in its
    beak.

We swore we heard the distant rumble of failure, or was it the armbones
of an angel flapping as the final feather loosened ... ?
None of your damn business! the mine foreman warned the guy who pointed,
so we kept our eyes averted, and rot — because we failed to stop
when the first shoe dropped — rot found a nailhole in the hoof,
a weak spot in the tunnel roof. *My god is dark*, thought Rilke.
The clouds dropped. Then the horse fell lame; it thundered hard.
Whatever we were ignoring grew larger, approaching. Like a raindrop.

THE PROCESS OF EXTRACTION[49]

The mine's exhaustion date is more than 20 years down the road ...[50]

365 days a year, round-the-clock, loss is taking place within the Empire Mine — miners sleep and eat at designated times, but the mine never sleeps, the mine never pauses in its chewing, the hole named *Empire* grows larger while you dream it: a red-dust dream of yellow trucks, each tire tall as a two-story house, moving in the landscape of the open pit, so far below they look like toys, then ants, then the ore-crush piles they carry are smaller than the sweet red crumb some yellow ant discovered on the far edge of your pillowcase, then no sense of scale at all — *that kind of loss*, where the ant-chewed hole widens into an Alice-in-Wonderland Mine, man-made wonder-of-the-world — remember that magnificent tunnel you were always digging to China as a child? Someone kept digging long after you lost interest — down! down, taking what they wanted as they went — down! down, to the heart-warmed mantlerock, to the stone arena where young men compete to woo the Other with brute force, twisting earth's arm until she cries *Uncle, Lover, Eat Me, Drink Me!* relinquishing such treasure to him as she alone should own, magnetite, hematite, taconite — down! down, to the labial entrance and the empty stope where a lover abandoned his workings for a redder vein — down! down, to the church of earthquakes and the caved-in basement and the bed of rusty rags from which Yeats said all our ladders start. *The Process of Extraction*, she begins, smoothing her picnic blanket over dusty grass, licking the lead of her pencil with deep concentration — then a dark door opens beneath her, a hole far deeper than any private loss. Where she falls, we fall. This is the Process of Extraction. These words are merely specimens from the shaft of our descent.

LIFEGUARDING

Remember how it ended? That summer at Cedar Lake
you were lifeguarding — the lake turned green, it came alive for me

& I couldn't help myself. Something under the surface spoke my name
flagellate. I cocked my head, held down my ear to hear

& under shimmer, blue-green under brilliant noon-shine,
I heard it eating sunlight, monk-amoeba or volvox, wetly

multiplying — just as something in the Athens Mine fed itself
on the glistening skin of our fathers, the sweat of their brows

transformed into manna, red mud, protoplasmic meaning.
I looked back at shore and it had gone distant, mythic,

a bright porch where I used to live on your beach towel,
half-vigilant — & you were the distant shape of something

I'd once loved. I dropped my chin into that living water,
then my lips, until it reached my nostrils, viridian,

then I drank it in, mucilaginous matrix, whatever greened that water
I swallowed willingly — chloroplastic, coenobitic, it knew my name!

I gave it license to my lungs, my tongue, I went down wet
and eyes wide open, I sensed emerging sentience, sloshing

photosynthesis. I offered sanctuary, I played host.
You weren't the only lifeguard.

ONE GOOD EYE

Maggie had only one eye, he had lost the other in an accident. While working with Maggie, they had a slice with curve, and the men running the tugger could not see the breast. Whenever this happened, one man would go to the outside of the curve and using his miner's lamp, would signal his partner (....) My father never forgot the day Maggie removed his glass eye and held it in his hand. He told my father to take the glass eye to the curve and he could run the tugger without my father's signaling.[51]

Hearing opera on the radio, I broke down
and wept: Aida.
I didn't understand word one but
hammered together a meaning
in my heart. Later, down't the Carnegie
I asked our librarian lady if maybe she'd explain it to me.
Sure, Mister Kai[52], she says, and she did.
She read me a synopsis. That's it, I said? That's all?
Disappointing, and I said so,
like Christmas after gifts were opened — the prettiest paper hid
wool socks, or when I finally met my childhood pen-pal,
a gal from Chicago — o I liked her so much better as I'd imagined.
Things best kept in a state of perhaps.
Possibly. Maybe. We'll see.

After that accident down't the mine
my partner Vaara begging for death
smashed beneath the slab, everyone expressed sympathy,
poor half-blind Maggie Kai, ah poor me! Perhaps.
Truth be told, I didn't mind losing that eye so much as you might think.
Saw plenty, I told them. Plenty 'nough shit for one life.
Some guys get stuck on Iron Street with their shot glass;
some guys keep shotguns oiled, binoculars at the ready
in the pickup, or hanging from a hook out t'camp
— gotta keep an eye on things, they say, how many points are on the bucks,
or (((retired & parking up on the rim))) who's got their old job
driving the giant dump trucks down in Empire.
They buy dimestore glasses for the fine print,

for captions, comics and obits. Me?
I say *maybe's* more interesting than a *fact.*
Death's in the details. Keep your details.
If you point at things, I'll nod politely,
I'll squint at the distance in blurry, honest wonder.
Sure, I'll say, no doubt about it, but I cherish doubt.

Here's my glass eye, I like to say if we're debating something,
slip it in and out of its socket, a leather ball in a mitt
— hold this for a minute, perhaps you'll
lemme see the world from over where you stand.

A matter of perspective.
Like that little Ilmiö girl[53] asked me, her first airplane trip
as we lifted into the air over Negaunee Airport, and Empire's tailing basins
flared into view, barn-red, liver-red. *Hey Mister Kai,*
she said, *when do we start getting smaller?*

COME SUNDAY, RUSTY, WE'LL BE DOWN IN THE BASEMENT AT SAINT TOM'S

watching the children put on their Passion play — an end,
finally, to their month of wonderings: *how long does it take to bleed*
to death? how tall a life-sized cross? which spices were used to marinate
the dead? how heavy the stone & who rolled it from the tomb?
Ah, well — we'll just follow the plot as best we can, knowing
how Jesus and Judas will be played this year by the Olson brothers,
those identical twins whose own mother admits she can barely tell the boys
apart, at that distance. *Though if you listen closely to the dialogue,*
she promised us yesterday, waiting in the checkout line,
it'll all make perfect sense.

RELEASING FLIES FROM THEIR FLY-BOTTLES

I have been urged to write a Complete History
of the Terrain in question — but how to begin?
Each morning, I stand at the fence of Caving Grounds
with a pencil in my right hand, my left hand
fondling the corroded padlock. Can we think our way within?
Per Bradley — *the present moment is the one in which the future, which flows*
    toward us, disintegrates into the past, that is, being is a ceasing to be; or, as
    Boileau said, (being is) without melancholy[54]
My mind extends her soft gray fingers
    under every fence, testing barbs, testing gates
        — curiosity cannot be kept at bay.
Friend, who shall I see about getting the key?

O world-renowned mines, we produced x billion of iron tons, an emptiness so
    intense
we bulldozed wide blocks of ourselves — Boom. Scram. Gone.

Per Agricola — *the fifth cause (of mine collapse) are fierce and murderous demons,*
    for if they cannot be expelled, no one escapes from them. The sixth cause is that
    the underpinnings become loosened and collapse, and a fall of the mountain
    usually follows; the underpinnings are then only restored when the vein is very
    rich in metal.[55]

Per Brodsky — *what's poetry but a review of the existing evidence?*[56]
Found wired to a fence, a mother's warning on a rusted baking sheet
in peeling yellow paint: *Caving Ground*

underpinned, upjutted & cliffhung
mined & slumped, shored-up, mucked-out, sold

⚒

After the cave-ins, word spread rapidly
"she's lost — have you heard? — ground's not stable up there"
Slumped. Until I earn a new human form and be transformed
"from caved rock back to marrow ..."[57]

⚒

What's visible: feral houses whelping litters of outbuildings:
garage, sauna, woodshed, toolshed, a greenhouse missing glass,
mossy outhouse, everything patched with whatever's handy:
corrugated scraps, advertisements printed on tin,
rough-cut planks winter-gray with bark left clinging,
particle-board distended by rain, chipboard falling into chips,
a map of wound & catch-as-catch-can.
Ma's darned socks. Pa's patched elbows.

⚒

Sunset when we pass
three nuns in full habit walking the narrow road to Empire:
the black-&-white of their garments silhouetted against the tailings,
their habits flapping like wings into the hot dusk.
Do you ever rub your eyes in disbelief?
I guess I am asking if you ever doubt yourself.

⚒

Living in another state we heard
my cousin sold grandpa's homestead
& I wanted to throttle him but we came back,
see, for a final look, & got the whole picture —
they'd held out long as they could while Empire approached
chewing up the neighboring hills,
explosions blasting closer & closer, sweet corn
shuddering, dishes falling from the shelves, the well-casing
broke, & then it was all over but the crying —

⚒

Reviewing a script concerning historic life on the Iron Range
we find this note inserted after slide 146 (Striking Miners on Parade):

- - - - - - - - - - -

To illustrate the last paragraph of the script dealing with the modern legacy
of Michigan's iron industry I recommend (a) professional photographer
take the following series of shots **in color**. This will provide a good contrast
with the black and white images which have dominated and will end the
presentation on a more up-beat note.

- - - - - - - - - - -

Further notes specify how the presentation should end:
Surviving Headframes
Abandoned mine buildings, perhaps overgrown with vegetation?
Water-filled pits, due to mine subsidence "Caving Grounds"
Conclude with Photo of Modern Ethnic Celebration!!

*Cornish Pasty Days! Da Yooper Tourist Trap Tent Sale! Da Yooper Great Trained Flea
Circus performing one night only at Pioneer Days! Finn-Fest! Folk Dances! Spaghetti
Night at St. Joe's Hall! Strawberry Days at the IGA! The Great Blueberry Bake-
off & Recipe Swap at Messiah Lutheran Women's Night, Hunter Stew Feast in Big
Bay, Voyageur Fur Fest, Outhouse Races! St. Urho's Mass! Mister History speaking at
Kaufman Auditorium — Live!*

Per Bordeau — *because trees in the Gribben Basin were buried beneath materials
carried by waters from a melting glacier, we now know that the Valders ice,
after possibly receding to the North Shore of Lake Superior, re-advanced*

The long-suffering Reader
has read many chapters of, let's be honest, melancholy details
& tragedies and such, so it is useful to switch tone now!
minor to major — something up-tempo as when the local band
accompanying coffins to the cemetery, after a mine accident,

slides from dirge to praise: *When the Saints Go Marching —*
O how I want to be in that number!

Guilty, thinking back.
I called in sick, you know.
I should have worked that shift.

All night, dark flies have been buzzing
up and down the cabin window, resurrected
by the heat of my woodstove: they believe
November will welcome them.

In Tractatus Logico Philosophicus,
Wittgenstein expresses his desire to "*Shew the flies*
the way out of their fly-bottles." When he died it was 1951,
another child had just died in the caving grounds
lured down, down, a bog fly into a pitcher plant's mouth.

Several varieties of carnivorous plants grow in our parts,
pitchers, fly-traps, sundews of various sizes;
formerly a great swamp existed at the Dead River's mouth
but with dikes and ditching, it was drained.
Note: read Wittgenstein again, if only to remind yourself
what may and may not be done with words.

We wrongly assumed
    whatever spirit once dwelled there
was gone.

Allyn digs a pitcher plant from that bog.
Perhaps he locates the same plant, each spring?
I shit you not, he keeps it in a pot on his cabin porch

like a petunia or a leashed dog, housebroken,
You feed them flies I suppose? I asked,
and he said, no, he feeds them hot dogs cut in chunks —
they thrive: hairy, green-veined. It seems wrong
how large they grow, beer-bellied men
in the bleachers of a game they once played.
They learn a taste for meat, these plants,
swell to great dimensions, red gullets,
some old mine boss in a three-piece suit
silver buttons bursting on his vest, hairy throat,
slippery talus slope that leads to a mine's deep stope —
Allyn, closing his camp each fall, *lets it go*,
meaning: he replants that meat-eater in the swamp.
You better wear long sleeves
when you enter our sunken places, friend,
    and carry a stick.

Do not believe, for a minute, that I am giving you
Truth, the sole truth. Nothing but.

Numerous sources
have been consulted, many long out-of-print
or outdated, most truth blasted to bits
or pulverized in great machinery,
exported, pelletized, clearcut, lost to subsidence.
        But I am telling stories
true in their outline, and I am saying something *about truth* —
how we personalize it with monograms,
His/Her, true-false, engraved dolomite, brass name tags,
family hymnals, tourism campaigns —*Pure Michigan!*
we buy and sell it. We dig the Idea up, wild and carnivorous,
feed it tinned meat, and abandon it back to peat. Unloved orphan
truth, polished rocks, stained postcards. Dear ma, dear sis,
dear Rusty, how history chews on us! stalks us,
                 consumes

    eludes

WATCH GREAT LADIES GET LOADED

I pity the industrial ports trying to reinvent themselves,
black bears chained & weary, forlorn, learning to dance
on their hind legs for tourists, upright in torn taffeta skirts,
foot-sore waitresses walking on heel spurs
where a billboard out along the main highway urges:
    Watch Great Ladies Get Loaded!

Down at the harbor, I've seen those freighter'd ladies
in port, shuddering stoic as their hulls thud the dock.
You'd get hammered too, I think, seeing the
taconite spouts drop down, relentless, entering —
how them ladies tip & right themselves & sink deeper,
resigned to carry every forced ton of ore poured into them.

EPISTLE OF LAURENTIA MAKI

How's the city treating you, Rusty?
How's your temp'ing down at the scrap iron company?
Steer clear of them giant dangling magnets, Son,
you got a head made of magnetite, sensitive as a compass

stubborn enough to scratch a knife,
you got a big heart like a red gob of hematite — don't
sell your days to anybody by the pound like a radiator.
Same old same old here, only growth industry's

the cemetery. Empire Iron laid off everybody
til end of August but at least there'll be less dust.
Last summer my sheets drying on the line turned ore-red,
my china hutch rattled like they were blasting moneyrock

in our yard. Division Street disappeared again,
same spot, more subsiding. More often than not, your Dad's
been drinking more brandy than coffee in his thermos.
Every night I hear that cemetery owl crying

Who cooks for you? Who cooks for you now?

UNDER OUR TOWN, AN ORACLE

It all begins with loss: a sudden lack-of-bearing,
compass fingers spin until they find the greed within us.
It all begins with rust: an egg of hematite plucked from an outcropping

and from the mine we dug to mark that holy spot an oracle was singing
Down! down — & down we went, where Dante flew for Beatrice,
where it might begin with iron after all, with Hematite, with him descending

as a blackened penitent into the grotto where he heard Iron singing,
a rusty bird in a cave of windy bells, where he worshiped, yes,
& left her weeping later. It begins with loss, a sudden bearing-

down of flesh, a lightless kiss as rock explodes or blasting
sticks discharge — just so, Iron crumbles at his fierce embrace.
It requires an iron fist, they say. Pure Hematite, poor mirror reflecting

the men who built Negaunee with stones they were stealing
from the altar of Iron. Didn't they see Her, watching in the darkness?
All their theft must end in rust, furious, when they're done ransacking

our cathedral. "Foundation, house, faith" — ferrous images we're painting
on a pale egg. Later, hungry: crack the shell and leave another mess.
It ends in profit-&-loss, iron abandoned for the cost of her extracting.
Further down the hole, a rusty bird guards her ruined nest, still singing.

As I said, it all begins with loss.

YOU ASK ABOUT IRON CONSUMPTION?

For a year after the Barnes-Hecker disaster
    Rutherford Wills worked a surface job
refusing to ever go down again;
    others claimed Wills
        moved away, changed his name, worked
security for an auto plant downstate,
    far from the holes we drilled for iron here.

⚒

The owl lifts into the night leaving only bony bits.
A hole, some fur, a lack.

⚒

According to one, Rutherford drank hard
    to keep memories drowned,
another said he never spoke again of *iron*
    forged a new life where no one knew
        how many names were lost
            & he never came back.
    No one guessed why he could not bear to see
young women passing, dressed in black.

⚒

You ask about Iron Consumption?
A daily dose. One-A-Day plus.
Why, our Durables demand it, our consumer goods
consumed by rust, consumed by us.
More accurate, perhaps, to say *iron consumes us.*

Throughout the report, Steel is necessarily spelled *steal*.

Mining Properties Fence (1986, 1987, 1989)	Number of Feet of Mesh Fencing	Number of Feet of Fence Repaired	Number of Feet of Barbed Wire
CCI:			
Athens Mine	450	0	512
Bunker Hill Mine	500	0	1083
Deer Lake Area, Superior Test Pit	200	0	600
Eric Pit	0	0	1,300
Jackson Pit	400	150	1,320
Lake Angeline	200	0	1,020
Lloyd Mine	50	0	0
Lucy Mine	200	0	40
Lucy Hill Area	600	0	2,700
Mary Charlotte Area	1,100	100	1,116
Mather "A" Mine	100	0	1,328
Mather "B" Mine	50	0	10
Michigamme Area	1,500	100	2,500
New York Pit	0	50	0
Patch Location (Negaunee)	500	0	300
Salisbury Pits	500	0	2,060
Tracy Mine Area	1,400	300	2,502
Republic Mine	400	0	0
Rolling Mill Area	300	100	0
U.S. Steal Properties:			
All Properties	0	1,200	100
Holmes Pit	142	0	0
Palmer Area (old shaft cave-in)	100	0	300
SEC 16 Pit	0	0	40
Inland Steal Properties:			
Barnes and Hecker Pit	140	0	0
Holyoke Mine Shafts	230	0	460
Rock Quarry, Marquette	2,500	0	0
Silverhead Mine Shafts	150	0	240
Book Property:			
SEC 28	430	0	100
Hanna Iron Company Properties:			
Cambria-Jackson Area (old shaft)	800	0	2,500
TOTALS	12,942 Feet	2,000 Feet	22,131 Feet

* The above properties were "fenced to prevent persons and/or domestic animals from accidentally falling into the shafts or open pits."

YOU ASK WHAT IS A MAGNETIC FIELD?

I reply, my child, we must first grasp basic principles of human desire — attraction, repulsion. Until 1820, the only known magnets were rocks called "lodestones" — magnetite, in truth, with space around the stone being a "field" in which unseen forces exerted strength and direction, *come-hither* and *I'm-outa-here*, a magnetic field analogous to the unhurried hours of love, openings in the terrain that beckon us, a footpath along the periphery, rejection. Be that as it may, we are asked to imagine a large ferrous object half-sunken in the earth, a cast-iron bathtub, the Virgin Mary[59] safe behind a locked iron grate, grieving mother in a half-subsided claw-footed shrine, holy meditation on man-cages or prisons, a last glance before the day-shift descended bodily into earth's bowels, giant magnet, orebody. What geologists term "rock formation" is called by others the fossilized body of the great trickster Nanabush, possessed of magnetic personality, famous for bawdy, godly pranks. The Anishinaabe say he collapsed in grief and turned to stone *when his sacred metals were revealed to white men*. His prone outline rises some thousand feet above Kitchi Gami; his great pine-covered chest no longer rises and falls, yet the fearful among us bow as our oreboats pass, even now. As for our own times and local customs, it was determined that an archival collecting program should actively solicit materials related to local mining including all areas of economic-cultural-social life, thus *this old fire-trap you see before you*. Our museum generates a magnetic field, pulling matter inward: three floors plus a basement stuffed like a Thanksgiving turkey with mine-issued scrip, curling sepia tones, tools and helmets and specimens and handwritten letters in many languages. Suffice it to say your father was a man of iron, a magnetic storyteller, your mother a whole tribe of copper ingots and loam. Sprinkle their remains here, over the earth. Metallic elements within their bones will return to the great Lodestone. Watch their ashes as particles align themselves, pointing the same direction, revealing an invisible magnetic field beneath your feet. In this way we are given names, we are given the route by which we reach what we seek, an arrow always pointing *down*.

CERTAIN THINGS YOU SHOULD KNOW ABOUT HYSTERESIS

Once magnetic field is applied to a piece of metal, the metal will "remember" the orientation of the magnetic particles.[60]

We tortured the elements to our will,
— iron torn open for the sake of possessing,
torn by picks, then dynamite, then monster-shovels
crushed to dust in rolling mills, heaped in stockpiles,
the leavings poured into tailing basins to settle out
as the blood libations Tiresias poured in his dug trench;
red particulate patience, broken in myriad portions.
Our hero, our ruddy servant Rusty —
> *my people believe he was killed because he took part in desecrating the Haunted Mountain, the home of the god of Thunder and Lightning.*

You mean the iron mine over at Negaunee?[61]

Hysteresis, yes. Of iron, ferrous, hysterical,
maybe ferocious or feral. Say what you wish
it all boils down to this: Iron remembers.
*The system that is being created has an inherent memory
of what has been done to it in the past (...)*

Shelley wrote of a time beyond the age of rust,
when Love will burst from unlit caves,
the timbered greed of our tunneling undone,
some good change rising from abused elements
as they collapse our greed, or merely forgive us
at the far end of our galaxy's industrial spiral
sprawl.

Iron will recollect our most nefarious acts.
~~It was sacred~~ It was elemental.
Fractured yet intact.

What happens when a magnetic field is applied to iron?
Iron "remembers" the magnet's orientation —
take a mountain range, ancient bedding material, continentals
ruptured by seismic shifts
    fused & bent & welded shut again,
earlier layers fired to boiling in volcanic kilns
and heaved to the surface in fault-vents,
    squeezed & uplifted & subsiding in their turn
sedimentary shifting to metamorphic
    — & through it all *oolitic grains of iron*
remain unturned, aligned to the magnetic poles as they *were*
    (& indicating *where*)
at the moment iron was born — ore's aboriginal alignment.

Ooh darling! *hysteresis* plants in us these oolitic grains,
love-embedded, muscle-memory in every fiber of the heart.
Hysteresis is Rusty, our rusty-toothed-lover-lost-oracle
forever saying: recollect me. Hell yeah. I remember.
Lean in, listen carefully! Love's iron stain cannot be rinsed.
Easier to learn than to forget & yet easier to forget than forgive —

> *The chief, to convince me, rubbed a specimen of ore on the oily back of my hand. It left a reddish-blue stain. Pulling a similar stone from the soft deerskin pouch around his waist, he rubbed it on my other hand. "The two stains were identical."*[62]

Iron remembers how it's done!

⚒

Even when the field's reversed, it takes brute strength
to undo the magnetism before iron shifts polarity.
Our bodies grow older, trussed or ruptured,
we trip, break hips, get plates or pins, we are advised
to take our own rehabilitation seriously — *seriously?*
pay attention t'yer own damn self, says Toivo.[63]
You looked outside lately?
                    Rust-bowl days descending.

⚒

At Auntie's Café ordering two eggs over easy
you asked at the counter, *How do I reach the scenic overlook?*
& the regulars snorted laughter, seeing the brochure,
Dat's rich, some tourism book promoted t'view from our rock piles, ha!
Wasterock mountains piled beside pits — there used to be
a road, sure, but it's all mine property now, private, locked gates.
You can't drive up there Ms. Missy, can't leer-peer down
into our holes or judge us, a textbook case of boom gone bust
but there's nothing to photograph, nothing to see.
You want scenery? It went that-away, with the economy.
Cook's pointing out at rusting train tracks.

⚒

I showed the county mine inspector the (tunnels) where we gone down
(on our vision quest) & discussed how dangerous these are for kids
maybe playing in them. He went to the Company & they decided
to close them permanently blowing them down
putting steel plates over.
We been busy here down at the Shaft Museum
25 to 30 people a day
everybody says They Like What They See!

⚒

It is a crime to cut a fence in caving grounds.
We must enter by the holes others have made.

⚒

All night, I hear women with gravel voices
and rust-red lips sing of oredocks, of November's drowned sailors,
of dirt roads leading to a wild inland sea. *Waiter, another bottle!*
We have too much iron, we must ship it elsewhere!
Iron! A toast to more iron!

⚒

As for the others in the
world — yes, there have always been bullies,

boys pulling wings off butterflies, hysterical women
shaking babies, Christians knocking penises off Greek statuary, etc.
We must never grow weary or think their dis/ease
will touch who we are, luminous, inside. As the Persian mystic Lala asks,
Do ashes leave a stain on a mirror?

⚒

Great Dipper at dawn. In autumn
I forget how thirsty I am
until I see your long silver handle
stuck down into the horizon like a pick-axe
where some stump or rock-fissure
holds it, dipper-up, bright petals
cupped to catch the dew.

⚒

According to "Alternatives to Protect Property Owners from Damages caused
by Mine Subsidences" *Appendix I: Michigan urban areas still subject to potential
subsidence problems resulting from underground mining operations include: Bessemer
Calumet Hancock Houghton Iron River Ironwood Ishpeming Negaunee* — and so
on and so forth, a shorter list if they just said which of our towns *were stable*, eh?

⚒

You undermined me, I went below
        your workings. You drilled and detonated
and now the surface world tips into your subsidence.
        There — going by,
        wasn't that our traitorous kitchen sink?
They speak of hitting bottom and I laugh,
        wasn't it Doc Williams who predicted
we shall not reach the bottom?
        Well according to the physicists
                even if you had an *impossibly deep hole*
                        you could not fling yourself down
                and die of *bottoming*
                                        hitting
rock-bottom.

No.

 You'd hit one wall or the other

 if only to prove the earth

 keeps spinning.

V.

the oldest macroscopic (visible to the eye) fossil — in the world. The fossils are of a primitive, filament-like relative of algae. Scientists have determined the age of the fossils to be 2,100,000,000 (2.1 billion) years old. The specimens are found in thin layers in one area of the (Empire) mine.[64]

Geologists explain the phenomenon as a tremendous hollow in a prehistoric seabed, little changed in shape since the time when tiny animalculae swam around and did whatever animalculae do to precipitate iron into the waters.[65]

The brain still fails to understand itself.[66]

QUESTIONS FOR READERS

1. Who's Rusty, anyway?

2. Under what conditions will iron float?

3. Describe the color of Empire mine tailings, seen from space?

4. Whose initials were carved into virgin pines in the Range, ca. 1846?

5. Why won't Rusty's perpetual motion machine ever work?

6. Test a dozen recipes for hastening rust.

7. For a liturgy in Caving Ground, which psalms?

8. Can you define *landscape fragmentation* in your own terms (a clinical paragraph, a diagram drawn on bar napkins, a howl)?

9. How did Mister Kai lose his eye?

10. Why couldn't we simply lower a rope and rescue them?

11. Where does the heart dwell in the Caving Grounds?

12. That sinking feeling — will it linger?

WE MAKE A CERTAIN MUSIC, ENTERING

There is the mine, there are the miners (...)
What always served and always serves is at hand.[67]

Entering the heavy door of the Negaunee antiques store
we pause at the swollen books marked FREE
and begin humming in the room of china, where each cup touched
rings clean against a serving plate, stained teapot, vase,
against mixing bowls in a rainbow of chipped glazes—
even toxic crimsons and cobalts — *for looks only* —
gaudy menageries of ceramic knickknacks: the dog-playing-fiddle
with a hollow middle meant for storing pennies, the rooster cookie jar
with lewd red comb and menacing talons, the chicken dish
with wings half-spread over butter-dish chicks ...

Notice how cleanly the hen's chipped neck lifts from her body
at the widest point, convenient, an invisible axe-line
that opens to reveal her stuffing cavity? Elsewhere, there are
music boxes, rooms of knives, the metal song of meals long-finished,
tarnished silver, bent spoons sleeping back-to-belly,
or blackened cook-sets, incestuous relics of early life at the camp:
copper families of infant tea-pots, the pancake-&-griddle twins,
mama soup-pans and daddy stew-kettles, all fire-beaten and isolated,
each inserted into the other for the sake of convenience.
O voyeurs! We love the room of canceled postage, lost meanings:

handwritten notes about snow and childbirth and husbands
down in the mines and over in the army and deep in the grave,
and signatures, mostly blurred or illegible, mostly forgotten.
If they were written in our language, it seems our duty to read aloud
these letters, dropped off by the Estate Sale officer
who rids himself of whatever doesn't sell between 10 am and 5 pm,
sold by the bag, by the truckload, sold for whatever they'll bring
by widows moving into efficiencies, by survivors busy with lives
in L'Anse, Lansing, Gladstone, by sons who ring the shop to say
hell, it's yours for the taking. It seems there's always someone
grieving at the back door, grateful to disinherit their cumbersome

bundles of memory, while someone else — someone like us —
leans into the front door, disturbing an iron bell that rings
with rusty pleasure. We make a certain music, entering:
willing buyers for the mold-soft box of all that's been, and gone.

POOR RUSTY, HE WAS ALWAYS SOMEBODY'S WEARY YOUNG HUSBAND BROKEN, DYING EARLY

You can't avoid him. Orangey-soda-bright-acid-pyritic
he puddles at your feet, omnipotent; Rusty's face on your beater pickup's
fender oxidizing into brittle lace, he was here from the start,
brittle photos of Rusty double-jacking in Jackson pit, 1856,
prying rock-pages open with his pick, holding drill or shovel,
carbide lamp, his black pupils swelling to fill the whole of his eyes,
o they swore he could see in the dark, that fellow!
               He's there, dumping cantilevered
ore-carts down in the Negaunee, compressed air in Blueberry,
electrified mucker in the Mather B, running the sump engine,
shouldering a widow-maker[68], and when the final shift
resurfaced, Rusty rode away atop the last orecar
sent downhill to waiting freighters; he swallowed darkness
in every drift he worked, unquenchable thirst that boy, he stood
your grandfather whiskey for whiskey in the Crow Bar
then steered the old man home, he's always been our dearest hope,
our North Star, sacrificial lamb, cherubic choirboy scrubbed for Mass
despite his fading black eye — & inside his work glove
a finger rock-shattered and bloody
                   O he kept going, poor Rusty,
he was always somebody's weary young husband
broken, dying early, dismissed heart-attack, trussed double-hernia
whistling cheery as the men descended single-file in Maas Mine,
into Athens Mine's dark maw, he was our virgin gulleted whole,
boy given night after night to Vulcan Mine, plaything for the town bully,
scapegoat, hero, Miner of the Year —
                          undaunted, tireless,
with a lift of his chin he'd nod to old blind Tiresias, the mine's night watchman
who nightly dug a ruddy trench in shattered hematite to pour the blood libation
fresh from Salo's Meats, raw aperitif to appease the ghosts
those ore-howls, horrible slobbering all the miners heard below,
rock-popping, tap-tapping, the gnawing noises,
a secret shivering certainty there was something deeper
than the lowest level, o, that was Rusty for you, whistling,
                             he shrugged it off,

he never wept, or wept openly, or maybe it was Rusty from the start,
him who made such unearthly sounds, him in the sobbing seams of our heart.

HOW TO EXIT THE CAVING GROUNDS

As an oreboat backing heavy-loaded
from harbor will turn to face a November gale
waiting beyond the breakwall: to face it full on,
nosing gust, brave in the beams

after the final page of a book is read
the leather-bound cover drops back, an unlatched window
we followed into the text closes with a thud behind us,
the topic shut, the oracle shuttered

leaving white cards tacked to logs for blazes,
pages made into folded arrows, sharpened end-rhymes
thumbtacking each phrase, taking the time to read
guide-signs nailed to timbers at intersections
or a surveyor's brass benchmark *monumented into concrete*
stumbled upon in the middle of a forest, wherever one tunnel
branches into two, pointing up, up! where
raises like ladders pierce doubt

imagining yourself the lone survivor, young
Rutherford who escaped Barnes-Hecker
as it fell in like a bad lung behind him
hand over hand up 800 feet to the surface
w/red mud foam swirling, chewing timbers,
each rung he climbed disappearing
in a vortex below his toes

with a hunch, a painful hump, as miners
left cramped Cornwall tunnels where

generations toiled so long they still walk stooped,
men bent to a single task, so endemic the stoop was thought to be
genetic, a defect peculiar to men.

⚒

a jigsaw puzzle missing a dozen near-
featureless pieces, identical twins, bland sands,
taconite pellets, pine boughs or flesh, generic ruddy rubble.
Scatter them behind you, offerings dropped to chaos:
They don't fit anywhere, never did. Quit trying to fill the gaps
& move on. Let someone else wielding tweezers
or a sledge hammer bang the mystery into place

⚒

as if in a vintage elevator "going up!"
waiting to be lifted, a ding of doors to open
then you'll step out night-blind
into a gleaming brass-&-glass ballroom,
wearing a tuxedo, blinking
into light —

⚒

writing your way up — words alone
will hold the roof

⚒

or ending with footnotes, crushed bones,
a mystery unsolved, instead of firm bottom
we find the bottom of another frayed rope.
Done, regardless. The narrative unspooled to a knot,
your bare feet dangling —

⚒

You meant to measure the Great Space below our city streets?
O, but Empire's empty veins go deeper than rods and rulers,

the Void goes on making more of itself for the pure joy
of *feeling itself measured.* Quit quantifying it

Leave, you ask? You dare?
Departing without advice or maps or comrades,
lacking consent! without two pennies to rub together,
tired of waiting, without the sense God gave geese!

with a scrap of Rilke taped to your helmet
or poised like a spade
                    through solid rock
and no space: everything is close to my face,
and everything close to my face is stone,
buried to the neck I believe you'll still hatch
further plots of escape

as words break along their bedding lines
— it runs through fingers
blast-shattered hematite, grammar-flour,
staircase hidden behind a library bookshelf,
a route to the surface, a shimmering text,
not a mere stack of pages bound by a clip —

I have heaped great hunks of blue iron
to surround my fire, which radiates heat back to me
all night. I am not procrastinating, only deferring
that sad morning when I ship you *product,*
fire-forged, boiled down, stapled

by which actions

may we escape the gravitational pull
of a subsidence zone?
Backfilling. Retracing. Daylighting — punching
roughly through. Prayer.

hoisted in buckets
worth more once you surfaced,
your soul yanked pure & twanging
from the body's shaft, musical chamber,
OR — carefully extracted
as if your only value is mineral tonnage, how malleable,
how tensile, how easily extruded, how well you'll conduct energy
or resist pressure

as breccia, angular fragments
broken and re-cemented together, lifted
with care, roped to a stretcher

as a black hole is left, fleeing inescapable center, Yes!
self-arresting amidst an in-flow of debris,
protecting your head as you're dragged up

as Lazarus, buried by cave-in
clawed to air by his partner's frantic digging;
the rest of the story a later fabrication, specularite
polished til it gleams,
resurrect yourself, I mean —

I'm leaving. I'm told there were holes wide enough for semi-trucks
to drive under the town, ten abreast; they came and went filled with ore,

there were ramps and ropes and rugged switchback routes,
air raises doubling as escape routes.
The longer you remain at depth the more you'll yearn to stay
(or like Hap after his rock-blackened lungs
were unable to bear atmospheric pressure at the surface,
longing to haul his La-Z-Boy down there)

or yet be pulled to the surface, miracle-rescue! Rusty leaving by bucket-sling
broken, or standing upright, stumbling out whole, blind as a worm under
sunlight, wriggling with delight as rain perfumes night

Forget it, resigned to darkness;
pale thing, a mushroom pony

or as Ariadne left thread where she turned
at each intersection of Doubt & Intuition —
leave a clue, I mean, a strand

and if after years of weary labor severed from surface life,
blackened slave forced to toil in the underworld of rocks,
Hephaestus handed you your wages:
a dirty flour-bag of iron filings,
what would you say? You'd weep, or beat him.
But surfacing, you won't believe
what pure gold you'll pull from the sack!
The sack was a lanced wound.
A hole in the seam of the sack, see?
Because of that flaw you escape intact.

RUSTY, DELIVERED

It came to pass then:
a decade after everybody believed him dead
Rusty returned to us in a red-hulled oreboat
a Greek name painted on her side, black horseshoe
he claimed meant Omega, *ending.*
Never contacting the upper harbor master
that foreign captain slid his ship
gently into our old harbor — abandoned oredock,
deep water toothy with rotten piers,
and foreign sailors deposited Rusty on the shore at dawn
passed out from their parting toasts,
ruddy-faced from sleeping on the freighter's deck
where hematite dust billowed from crevices
and lodged in his face's every seam:
he seemed an old man now, Rusty.

No spouts dropped to fill her,
nothing rumbled. Omega left as she'd come,
in fog. A fisherman entering his shack of drying nets
shook his head as if he'd seen a ghost-ship —
the old Paavo B. Tiresias, filled to bursting
back in those money-days when freighters entered here,
he imagined the high trestle still towered over Front Street
with taconite pellets hailing down, orecars rattling.
Then he saw Rusty's body on the dock,
a heap of rags that breathed, and he blinked, and crossed himself.
Where'd our boy been, Pride of Irontown, Prince of Ruins,
in what dark ports delayed? *Hey!*

Fog shifting to a mist, Rusty opened his raw eyes,
saw he was home and hailed. The rain bled away red years from him,
he raised his arms — *I am back among pines, I am delivered!*
he shouted to the gulls, who reeled from his smile
and spiraled up into another wool-gray day.

CERTIFICATE OF CAVING GROUND & MINE RESCUE

This is to certify that (your name) _____ _____
has explored the phenomenon of Caving Ground and learnt the use of Mining Rescue Apparatus. During the course of training, the Reader has navigated underground workings and submerged environments and demonstrated skills required for scenarios including but not limited to surface subsidence, rock-burst, water influx, unanticipated fall of ground, shaft collapse, cable snap, tunneling through rubble, faults and deformations, drinking water contamination, explosives handling, shockwave-induced memory loss, hard labor in noxious or irrespirable gases, self-arrest on fractured slopes, generational despair (*& them who won't or aven't learnt are doomed to repeat t' course!*)

Date: _____
Signed: Stan Hywet[69], Inspector

AN EDUCATIONAL PROGRAM CONCERNING MINING

Here's how it works, our leader says, picks people from the audience at the Iron Mining History Museum, sorts us by height, makes everybody lift their arms straight out in the air. Our aligned row of necks and our upright spines he calls *the Mine Shaft.* Our parallel lifted arms he calls Drifts on Consecutively Deeper Levels. Some mines, he tells us, went down a hundred levels, several thousand feet or more. The tallest fellow's head is the shaft house, his ears are iron wheels grooved for hoisting cables. He is ordered to *whistle & squeal & screech.* Fathers are chosen to use their bare hands as *shovels & picks.* The rest of us wait with arms upraised, standing there like we're surrendering. Our leader tells us to send up iron, we must use our hearts, arteries, biceps, stoop and lift, shovel and fill, hammer and blast. *Are you feeling it? It's hard work, a messy business, ore!* A few of our fathers are told to lay down on the floor now, injured or killed, crushed, and our leader runs through tossing something between our feet, toy mice made from scraps of rabbit fur. *Rats, everywhere you looked there were rats!* he yells. He's excited now, blowing red dust over us, powdered blood meal. We inhale it and cough. We're sweating now, shouting and squealing and blasting and shoveling and hoisting, waving arms and stooping, red dust caking on wet skin. The audience looks uneasy. *You're the Location, the neighborhood around the mine,* he tells them. He throws red dust on them. *See, red was orebody, red was labor.* He says *men died wheezing, red lung.* He says *Millions of Tons. Billions! Fame & fortune! Are you listening? Are you getting this? Laundry drying on the line turned pink, we took our rock and turned it into Money!* A girl in the audience is weeping, a woman objects, but too late. *Proud history,* says our leader. He gives our fathers scrip, takes it back again. He sells them candles and blasting caps. He plants our mothers here and there, he calls them *virgin pines,* makes them chant *Pines hold up the Mines!* — limbs jutting, limbs akimbo, tossing wild hair, snapping under pressure. The leader says we must cut down our mothers to make more mining timbers. *I didn't ask for this,* whimpers a boy covered with dust; the boy and his grandmother coughing, rubbing eyes. *We must think about what Industry needs.* The leader tells the children to join hands now, teaches them to sing, *There's a Treasure in the Ground, Dig it Out, Dig it Out! There's a Treasure in the Ground — Dig it Out!* They repeat it, jumping up and down in their seats, coughing and stomping their feet while we, a mining machine made of fathers and mothers and children — *Dig it Out, Dig it Out* — go on shoveling and grinding and sweating, shuddering and blasting and suffering. *Dig it Out!* — not sure how we got into this or how we make it stop.

ACKNOWLEDGMENTS

Deepest debts are owed to dozens of folks who endured my fumbling, earnest questions as I gleaned the historical details embedded in these poems. I am grateful to everyone who shared personal stories of their lives in Negaunee and Ishpeming, and memories of the Caving Grounds, including Ann Marie Sarkela (1935-2021), Aili Koski (1921-2008), Ernie Ronn (1925-2004), Geno Beltrame (1908-2002), Gail Sipola (1921-2012), John Violetta (1919-2003), George Junior Temple, Lila Green (1911-2005), Marie Rogers (1934-2021), Merle Oien (1921-2012), Rollie Juchemich (1925-2009), Rudy Kemppainen (1931-2016), Tsu-Ming Han (1924-2005), and C. Fred Rydholm (1924-2009) — a rare human library. Their words live on in these poems.

I am also indebted to the editors of these publications, where selections from *The Caving Grounds* first appeared, some in far earlier versions —

"A Field of Mudswallows," "Come Sunday (We'll Be Down in the Basement ...)," and "How the Abandoned Lands Speak" appeared in the anthology *33 Minnesota Poets* (Nodin Press, 2000).

"A Pocket Guide to Caving Grounds" appeared in *Stoneboat*.

"After Iron's Boom Goes Bust" appeared in the anthology *Superior Voyage* (Gordon Publications, 2022).

"Barnes-Hecker Mine Disaster as a Schrödinger's Box" appeared in *Untethered*.

"Certain Things You Should Know About Rusty" appeared in *The Maynard*.

"Come Sunday (The Dog of His Thoughts ...)" appeared in *100 Words on Gardens* (University of Iowa International Writing Program, 1998).

"Miracle in the Museum of Iron Industry" appeared in *Queen Vic Knives* and in the anthology *Superior Voyage* (Gordon Publications, 2022).

"Now Playing," "Miss Iron Range Sings Reba," "Father Varamäki's Homily," "Poor Rusty, He Was Always Somebody's Weary Young Husband Broken, Dying Early," "Olson Bros. Waste Management," and "An Educational Program Concerning Mining" appeared in the anthology *Yooper Poetry: On Experiencing Michigan's Upper Peninsula* (Modern History Press, 2024). The poem "An Educational Program Concerning Mining" was nominated for a Pushcart Prize.

"The Process of Extraction" and "We Make a Certain Music, Entering" appeared in *Passages North*.

"Under Our Town, an Oracle" (previously "Villanelle for a Negaunee Oracle") appeared in *Explorations* (University of Alaska-Juneau) and the Ambassador Poetry Project.

Finally, thanks to the staff and rich collections of the Peter White Public Library, Marquette Regional History Center, Cliffs Shaft Iron Mining Heritage Site, Michigan Iron Industry Museum, Negaunee Historical Society, Cornish Pump Museum, Iron Mountain Mine Tour, Quincy Mine Historic Tour, Tilden Mine Tour, and the Cedar Tree Institute, which hosted the first reading of this work.

Critical support for this sprawling project was received from The Loft Center for Writers, the McKnight Foundation, the Jerome Foundation, and the Bush Foundation.

ENDNOTES

1 Rumi, translation by Coleman Barks.

2 Contents may have settled.

3 Arthur Koestler, "The Three Domains of Creativity" from The Concept of Creativity in Science and Art (Martinus Nijhoff Publishers, 1981).

4 U. S. Dept. of the Interior, National Park Service, Pictured Rocks Official Map and Guide (Washington: GPO, 1992).

5 William Stafford.

6 shaft *n.*=[From the Latin scapus shaft, stalk] 1 : the long handle of a spear or similar weapon 2 : a sharply delineated beam of light shining through an opening 3 : something suggestive of the shaft of a spear or arrow especially in long slender cylindrical form: as in a tree trunk or obelisk 4 : a vertical or inclined opening of uniform and limited cross section made for finding or mining ore or ventilating underground workings (as in a cave) 5 : harsh or unfair treatment (getting the shaft).

7 exhaustion *n.*= 1 : fatigue, lassitude, enervation, weakness, debility, weariness, 2 : depletion of mineral resources, consumption of an orebody.

8 Finnish words — *vaara* means "danger" and *mäki* means "hill" translated by Teppo Pihlajamäki.

9 caving grounds   n.= euphemisms include: barrens, brownfields, gardens of loss, failed zones, subsidences, caving zones, displacements, Private Property, zones of tension, yielding ground, seemingly innocent meadows.

10 Diane Sautter, "Lake Superior Deva."

11 Arthur H. Robinson and Barbara Bartz Petchenik, *The Nature of Maps: Essays toward Understanding Maps and Mapping* (University of Chicago Press, 1976).

12 Burt Boyum, Chief Geologist, "A Paper on The Marquette Mineral District Michigan, Presented to the Conference on Lake Superior Geology National Science Foundation Sumer Conference" (Ishpeming, MI: Cleveland-Cliffs Iron Company, 1964).

13 "United States Bureau of Mines Studies Moon Mining Under Research Grant" (...) the Bureau of Mines has begun looking into the problems that may be encountered in mining on the moon ... The program isn't aimed at finding new sources of metals and minerals for use on earth, but at opening up sources of supply for the time when man begins to inhabit the moon ... Experts are enthused by the project but concede moon mining may not be so easy as it sounds. Walter E. Lewis, Director of the Minneapolis Bureau of Mines Research Center where the program is under way, says 'the extremes of environment will probably require an all new mining technology. Mere modification will insufficient.'

14 Interview with Ernie Ronn.

15 Nennius.

16 B. T. Shaw, "3.10" from *This Dirty Little Heart.*

17 Holmes Boynton, *Icelandic Folk Tales.*

18 H. Gregory, "Introduction to In The American Grain."

19 Thomas McGrath, *Letter to an Imaginary Friend.*

20 After Margaret Atwood, "The Landlady."

21 Ernie Ronn, *52 Steps Underground.*

22 dries *n.*= industrial changing room and bathhouse. The mining companies built dries — huge showers in which miners could stash their clean clothes, and wash away some of the ore dust before they headed home, maintaining a cleaner image for the mine.

23 Phil Strong, "The Mesabi." *Holiday Magazine*, July 1950.

[24] Johann Wolfgang von Goethe, Den Vereinigten Staaten. "Amerika ... Hast keine verfallene Schloesser. (America ... you have no ruined castles)."

[25] Robert Travers, *Laughing Whitefish*.

[26] Louis Jenkins, "Iron."

[27] June E. Rydholm, "Geno, My Father" (interview 2002).

[28] Ibid.

[29] Tiresias *n.*= A blind prophet changed (by a prank of the gods) into a woman midway through life.

[30] Robert Bly, "One Source of Bad Information."

[31] *History of Northern Michigan* (Central Michigan University).

[32] Statement by Mike Prusi, former Michigan Senator.

[33] Michigan DNR, *Porcupine Mountains Wilderness State Park Visitor's Map Guide* (Lansing, MI: DNR, 1990).

[34] Thurston Smith Jenkins, *The Days of Mines*.

[35] Renee Prusi, "NHS students to honor caving ground victims." *The Mining Journal*, May 29, 2001.

[36] Dana Gioia, "Unsaid."

[37] Thurston Smith Jenkins, *The Days of Mines*.

[38] Finnish proverb: "If whiskey, tar or sauna does not help, death is certain."

[39] Thomas Merton.

[40] Bill Bryson.

[41] Reba McEntire, from "Turn on the Radio."

[42] fossil *n.*= organic cells replaced with mineral materials.

[43] Letter from Melvin Paden cited in *Mining Camps Speak: A New Way to Explore the Ghost Towns of the American West* (Beth and Bill Sagstetter, 1998).

[44] John Donne.

[45] "Basics for the Non-Scientist." TRIUMF website, Canada's National Laboratory for Particle and Nuclear Physics.

[46] Robert Travers, *Laughing Whitefish*.

[47] "Winnie-the-Pooh and the Pebble Hunt."

[48] "About suffering they were never wrong, the old Masters" is a line from W. H. Auden, "Musee des Beaux Arts."

[49] extraction *n.*= ancestry, origin, descent v.= the work of removing, excavating, wrenching, uprooting, tooth-pulling.

[50] Dale Hemmila statement, Cleveland Cliffs Natural Resources Public Relations.

[51] Interview with Ernie Ronn.

[52] *Kai* — Finnish word meaning perhaps, translated by Teppo Pihlajamäki.

[53] *Ilmiö* — Finnish word meaning "phenomenon" as translated by Teppo Pihlajamäki.

[54] Jorge Luis Borges.

[55] Georgius Agricola, *De Re Metallica*, translated by Herbert Clark Hoover and Lou Henry Hoover.

[56] Joseph Brodsky, "Speech over Spilled Milk."

[57] Margaret Atwood, "Eventual Proteus."

[58] Information from the *Annual Report of Inspector of Mines* (fiscal years 1986-1989) of W. C. Maki, Marquette County Mine Inspector.

[59] After a photograph by Camilo Jose Vergara.

[60] Gregor Hohpe.

[61] Robert Travers, *Laughing Whitefish*.

[62] Ibid.

[63] *Toivo* — Finnish name, meaning "hope."

[64] Tsu-Ming Han and Bruce Runnegar, "Megascopic eukaryotic algae from the 2.1-billion-year-old Negaunee Iron-Formation, Michigan." *Science*, Volume 257, July 1992.

[65] Phil Strong, "The Mesabi." *Holiday Magazine*, July 1950.

[66] Anne Hart, winner of a 2002 Ig Nobel Prize for Neurobiology, asked for a concise seven-word summary of her topic.

[67] Walt Whitman, "Song of the Broad Axe."

[68] widow-maker *n.*= [mining slang] Compressed air-drill, used to bore holes for dynamite in hard rock mining. Rock often flew back, injuring the man holding the drill. Prolonged inhalation of the fine rock dust caused the deadly lung disease, silicosis.

[69] literally *Stone Quarry*.

ABOUT THE AUTHOR

Kathleen M. Heideman is the author of *A Brief Report on the Human Animal* and *Psalms of the Early Anthropocene*. A writer/artist/environmentalist working in Michigan's Upper Peninsula, she has completed residencies with the National Park Service, watersheds, research stations, private foundations, and the National Science Foundation's Antarctic Artists & Writers Program. Drawn to wild and threatened places, she works to defend them as a board member of the Upper Peninsula Environmental Coalition. Heideman received the "Freshwater Heroes" award from Freshwater Future, and has a handful of Pushcart nominations — her other hand is full of moss. Curious woman.

YOOPER POETRY SERIES

Michigan's Upper Peninsula—a remote region, blessed by water and boreal wilderness, sparsely populated, battered by a history of economic boom-and-bust—is represented by a growing body of literature, particularly poetry. The Yooper Poetry Series (YPS) spotlights the diverse work of poets with a strong connection to the U.P., those who have been shaped and transformed by the experience of life off the beaten path.

Yooper Poetry: On Experiencing Michigan's Upper Peninsula
Edited by Raymond Luczak

A Bigfoot Bestiary and Other Wonders
Martin Achatz

The Caving Grounds
Kathleen M. Heideman

Available in paperback, hardcover, ebook, and audiobook
via Modern History Press
modernhistorypress.com/YPS

www.ingramcontent.com/pod-product-compliance
Lightning Source LLC
Jackson TN
JSHW012005291224
76211JS00001B/2

*9 7 8 1 6 1 5 9 9 8 4 5 6 *